Walk
Your Path
A Magical Awakening

GW00691322

JESSICA MARIE BAUMGARTNER

GREEN MAGIC

Green Magic
53 Brooks Road
Street
Somerset
BA16 0PP
England

www.greenmagicpublishing.com

Designed & typeset by K.DESIGN
Winscombe, Somerset

ISBN 9781916014022

GREEN MAGIC

Contents

Introduction

Call me a witch if you like. I have been called many things. My heart warms to words like: Pagan, magic, and personal energies. If that makes me a witch in your eyes, so be it.

My path, like many of yours, is a winding route filled with rocks and pebbles. Trees and bushes have blocked the view at times, but metaphors grow old and rot away. I have always allowed the wind to blow me in the right direction (literally and figuratively). The Gods know me well.

Raised by a woman who believed all faiths to be connected, I craved theological understanding. My self-imposed studies showered me with information. Holy books and philosophy texts provided some great truths, but the balance presented me with well-drawn lines. I crossed a specific boundary when I left behind monotheism to embrace the male and the female aspects of the Gods.

My mother's Catholic upbringing influenced me in ways she never expected. The roots led further than Christ, back to a time when humans worshiped the land and understood the true meaning of sacrifice. I clung to "the old ways." They danced with me.

The beliefs my mother passed on never changed. "Religion is a man-made concept," she often said. I doubt she will ever know how correct she was, or what a service she offered me by allowing my spirit to find its proper way.

By eighteen I was studying Scott Cunningham and Gerina Dunwich, but it was not until I went shopping and found a curious pop-up book sale that Sybil Leek's, "*Diary of a Witch*," spoke to me.

Books are sacred. They always will be.

My habit of closing my eyes and sliding my fingers over the bindings lined on bookshelves often led me to new ideas. This time I was graced with an old copy of Sybil's great story. The bright red cover held no pictures or even the title. It sat blank in my hands, but the pages screamed for attention.

I bought the book for much less than it was worth. Her story is one all spiritualists should read. She is a constant guide and reference. Learning about her connection to Aleister Crowley disturbed me at first. Like many, I believed him to be an evil man. I couldn't understand how someone so good could be connected to such a brute.

Since then I have learned better.

History is full of misunderstandings. Doing more research on the man has lifted my concerns. Books often aided me in learning the opposing side of all great feuds/fears. Pagans and witches often know the bitter truths of being misunderstood. We harbor a deep history. It lurks in our past.

My Pagan roots came calling long before I learned how far back my family tree tangled itself in it, sprouted from things left out of books.

Like all writers, I sit before a manuscript for many reasons. Writing about my beliefs offers relief, understanding, power and guidance. I first began publishing articles and essays for *The Witches' Voice* and got a piece into *Circle Magazine* before it was shut down. Since then I have found a community (starting where I live in Saint Louis) that reaches all the way around the globe. I met Selena Fox at the annual Pagan Picnic, and I have sold my Pagan children's books in numerous cities.

This book was born from all of those experiences, but it mainly sprung from you. The letters I received and continue to get from other Pagans and people of all faiths (one of my first readers, a Christian priest on the East Coast of the USA). They hold many questions. I am no expert, but I try to answer as best I can.

I have practiced the art of "knowing thyself" for a couple of decades now. Magic and spiritualism are my life. Connecting with nature and its creatures is my world. Focusing my energies to create balance is a never-ending goal.

I am a witch. I am a Pagan. I am everything, just as you are.

Here are my answers and here is my tale.

Getting Started

From a young age the wild called to me. Forests and trees reached with limbs that cradled me into their world surrounded with animals. I perturbed my mother to no end coming home caked in mud and bug bites. Each bruise on my legs was a medal.

Tree climbing excursions allowed my sister and I to look inside our second-floor bedroom window from the comfort of sap and bark. Fresh pines became a quick favorite. They reminded me of nobler times. Instead of dwelling on my father's drinking or the temper it inflamed, nature sat ready to show me his more charming side when he donned the cap of a country philosopher.

I grew from a pudgy tomboy into a teen thick with a thirst for more than most high school dramas. There were plenty of those. Acne, dating woes, and struggling to find a diet that fit my broad frame curtained the world, but they could easily be swept away by hiking or swimming. The gods I grew to love weren't living in a church or synagogue. History lived there. Humanity.

The best place to find the voice of creation came on remote trails. In state parks, or on private property that begged for trespassing. At fifteen, my home life left a lot of gaps in my development, but the sky was always there.

When my father's drinking and inability to be faithful to my mother finally convinced her to file for divorce the trees still grew, the birds still sang. He moved out and the fog lifted, until a young friend of mine was murdered by his father.

The gruesome details terrified me and haunted my mother. My dad's own changeable personality seemed too connected. My friend's father came to his home and killed his mother, his step-father, him, and his baby brother before committing suicide.

Never before had tragedy tested my faith, but this was too close to my heart, my life. It sparked a new quest.

What did I really believe?

Who was I?

Why did I exist and what was the point of all of it?

When not chasing the Sun's rays, books had lent their strength. No matter what illnesses swept in, their pages offered comfort over pneumonia, the flu, and strep throat. They had been a lifeline to other perspectives, wisdom. Now I turned to them for guidance.

I had read the Bible at nine. Six years later I found myself searching through Buddhist, Hindu, and Taoist texts. They offered some insight but did not speak with as grand a voice as I hoped. Nothing matched the depths of a forest. Nowhere did philosophy or theology compel me to devote myself entirely. They did give me a beginner's course in meditation and self-awareness, but I needed more.

It was like talking to myself but more socially acceptable. Conversing with myself had been a perfect way to enter new situations with confidence. Those lone back-and-forths led me to find inner peace during many struggles. Meditation brought light to what I was learning.

My search for answers grew, but life got harsher. I suffered an abusive first love, neglect at home, and a suicide attempt. Survival became a necessity and adulthood beckoned me before my high school years ended.

Like everyone in life, I longed for understanding. The common question of, "What kind of God would allow this?" plagued me. I was young and selfish. I had much to learn.

A surge in movies and books about witches ranged through my generation at the right time and my research led me to join the rising trend. Instead of dabbling irresponsibly, I found a world of possibility, opportunity, and knowledge.

One of my friends who claimed hereditary links to the ways of old inducted me, my sister, and another friend into a new coven. Our quartet mediated together, cast simple spells, and worked with our energies. Always eager to learn, I was enchanted at first, but then her ego got the better of her.

It was nothing like the cinematic gold of the movie, "The Craft." She just began pitting the rest of us against each other.

During that time, we decided to explore an old abandoned nursing home. I had been once or twice. It definitely held a presence or some kind of eerie spirit. The walls were marked with strange ritualistic outlines and someone had lit candles inside a pentagram. Going with the members of my coven magnified each guarded instinct. The dark called to me. The dead fireplace in the main hall stared with ire.

We shuffled along the creaky floor together giggling like children, but when we neared the basement steps, my stomach wretched. I don't remember how we left. My sister and the rest of the coven got me out of there, but I could barely move. Once they collectively got me into the car, drove me home, and took me back to the safety of my basement room at home, our priestess tried chanting. She lit candles around me, but I felt no warmth.

I couldn't speak. I couldn't move my face. The catatonic state left me trapped in my head. I drifted through a hazy consciousness where caring no longer existed.

My sister sat in front of me. "Jessie! This isn't funny." She slapped me hard across the cheek.

I blinked. I wanted to respond and hit her back, but I couldn't move.

Our priestess tried an energy transference. She took two stones and placed one in my hand. She gave the other to our other friend and had her sit with me and hold my hand.

"I need you to focus on the rock," she said.

Something about the rock brought clarity. That connection, that bond to nature reminded me who I was. I focused. My body grew hot. My breath quickened. After time immeasurable I gasped. "What the hell was that?"

No one could fully explain, but I learned to be careful with everything after that. Spells and magic are never to be taken lightly.

Soon afterward our coven disbanded. My sister lost interest, we lost touch with the other friend, and our priestess devolved into self-righteousness.

All I had left was myself; myself and the Gods. I could feel them in everything. I saw their faces in trees and bushes. The smiling light of a goddess watched me from flowers, and colorful shrubs.

Whatever journey had started, I could not abandon it.

I again turned to books and listened to the wind. It grew louder and sent me sailing for more answers.

Books

Certain authors voiced truths I had lived. Scott Cunningham's, "*Wicca: A Guide For The Solitary Practitioner*," gave me the basics and I devoured many of his works including these main three:

> *The Complete Book of Incenses, Oils, & Brews*
> *Earth, Air, Fire & Water*
> *Living Wicca*

His approach offered guidance but also freedom. He lent encouragement and intelligence. I took my studies very seriously and read as many authors as possible, but I hadn't even begun. I was still attacking the local new age stores and the spirituality section of Borders Books (back when they still existed).

The more I read, the better I controlled myself and my emotions. I tested out spells for practice but took a no tolerance stance toward love spells and workings aimed on others without their knowledge.

A luck spell here. A confidence spell there. Everything I did was mainly for self-improvement.

Gerina Dunwich grew to be another favored source. She had the credit of being born into the old religion. The term hereditary witch rang in my ears. This was a woman whose family had thrived and passed down magical knowledge through the generations. Two of her books especially resonated best with me:

> *Exploring Spellcraft*
> *Wicca Craft*

In the style of Cunningham, she displayed wisdom like a friend offering secrets. Her books inspired me to carefully create my own spells and they almost always worked. Instead of buying numerous oils, lighting a rainbow of colors, and littering the air with too much incense, I found that my ability to create change with thought alone came with whatever ceremony I best connected with.

It was not the spell itself that mattered; it was my belief in the spell. The Moon's phases held more sway over outcomes than whether or not I held an amethyst crystal at a ninety-degree angle in front of burning sage. Stones did hold power, yes, but they were not the power itself. The power was in my connection to everything present. Mind-over-matter.

That reminded me of my grandfather. My mother's dad was a tough World War II vet. He had earned a purple heart fighting the Nazi's in the French countryside. He did not often speak of the struggles. The only war story he ever liked telling me was about how they used to poach cows from the farmers and accepted cheese from them even though it went against orders.

He chose to remember the funny stuff. Like accidentally missing a cow and having a bullet ricochet and echo until his buddies thought they'd all be reprimanded. The cheese had been his only true comfort in a fox hole. It blocked his bowels for days and minimized messes as there were no bathroom breaks or convenient bathrooms nearby.

Grandpa was a real man. Tall and broad shouldered, he believed in boundaries. He believed in rules. But something else sparked in his deep brown eyes.

Under his thinning grey hair, his head held more than just liver-spots. He taught me about the power of visualization.

I was a wild kid. Full of energy and a love of sport, I got into trouble for knocking into things, and sometimes people. Grandpa often yelled at me in my younger days, but sometime around puberty he recognized that I was growing up and managed to teach me something I would later use in every magical practice.

13

He sat at the kitchen table with his newspaper and his coffee. He always sat at the kitchen table with his paper and his coffee. But instead of barking at the TV news, he was ready to teach. "Try and knock my hand out of your way." He turned his chair toward me and held out his arm.

"Is this a trick?" I raised an eyebrow and bunched up my mouth.

"Just try it." He winked.

I pushed his hand away.

"Now, try again." He made a fist and stared ahead.

I pushed it, smacked it, leaned all my fat body's weight on it.

He tapped his forehead. "It's all up here. Now, put your hand out."

I sighed and held it out. He knocked it away.

Then he stared at me with his deep chestnut eyes. "I'm going to hit it again, but you will stop me. Want to know how?"

I nodded.

The corners of his weathered mouth twitched. "Imagine you are holding the heaviest bucket filled with water. Your arm is weighed down. It cannot move."

I laughed and he frowned. "I want you to really try this, Jessie." He scowled.

I took a deep breath and closed my eyes. When I opened them, he gave my hand a hard knock and I blocked it.

Grandpa was no magician, but like most grandparents he had some kernels of wisdom. It's amazing how something so simple can take hold of you and root itself into your character, help you draw from it for years.

Visualization is the main ingredient of magic, inner peace: power. If you can focus your mind and see the future, you can create it. Meditation is the exercise of controlling the mind and potentially allowing the spirit to reach further than the brain. It can be used to clear thoughts away or to increase energy to prepare for spell-work.

My mind is a like a cannon, constantly shooting. Rapid thought is something many suffer, especially in the technological age, but that cannot be used as an excuse. I used what my grandfather had taught me when I started mediating years later. At first I spent hours trying to force my head to fix itself. All that did was get me stuck on recording how many thoughts I had per min.

That exercise consisted of tapping a piece of paper every time your thoughts shifted while sitting with a stopwatch (yes, before the cell-phone boom). I averaged fifty-four different shifts per min. I effectively thought about fifty-four different things in sixty seconds.

I needed a better method.

For me, meditation comes best before bed. I found it worked best if I lay down after talking to myself and the Gods and just cleared my mind and drifted before sleep. I've heard some people advise against this because you can fall asleep unguarded, but I never did even though I fall asleep fast.

Once I embraced this technique, things came together. I also found links to my childhood in everything. When afraid of death or aliens as a child I would pray. When I studied Buddhism I found myself imagining a force field around my body. I utilized both of those ideas. They complimented my new revelations.

Instead of fearing what lay in the dark, it was my own inadequacies that left me quivering under my sheets. To remind myself that fate is its own beast, I would visualize a blue light starting in my chest. It always expanded on its own, growing until it slid down my legs, up my arms, and coated my body in a glow of healing light.

I later realized it was a simple protection spell, one that I still use today and have taught my children as well. It was this spell that led me to find my own talents in healing. I had always adopted stray animals and worked to tend the injured. I found new purpose in mending my aches and pains with magic. I extended this to only those closest to me with their consent and the result was always positive.

I fancied myself as a healer and landed a job as a veterinary assistant after high school. Playing nurse to sick animals was one of the greatest joys of my life. I felt that they didn't often squander kindness. My connection to nature followed me. I always sought refuge in the woods when things got tough. When the weather brushed me off, winter sheltered me with books.

My childhood habit of walking through the library with my eyes closed and stopping to read whatever book my hand landed on brought me to that great source: Sybil Leek. A random used book fair set up in the mall I frequented. Bored of the indoors I happily skipped over to the unknown shelves. I dragged my fingertips over numerous bindings and stopped. When opening my eyes I found a blank red bound book staring back at me.

The plain cover kept my attention. Something inside screamed to be read. My heart felt a tug and I opened the worn copy of a witch's diary, or so it said: *Diary of a Witch*

The first sentence took hold of me and I didn't care what it cost, that book was mine before I bought it. It belonged to me. I could feel it.

The author, Sybil Leek, detailed her life as a hereditary witch. From her enchanting childhood to her ageless grandmother and the years beyond, I finished it in one day. It was not a hefty read but contained more information than I paid for. How could a cheap second hand book hold so much meaning?

The older the book, the more useful it is, I've since found.

Sybil Leek is a pillar of Pagans and witches. Her life was controversial but also surrounded with awe and strength. Her connection to Aleister Crowley struck me at first. I had heard the name vaguely referenced as a dark no-no among white witches.

In Leek's autobiography she spoke of him as a loving uncle who adored nature, philosophy, and humanity. It was his followers and their misdeeds that she wrote of sometimes committing heinous acts, not him. I wondered if he was a misunderstood figure, a scapegoat for Christians and others who held a bias against polytheism.

Despite this curiosity it was not until I fell in love with my second husband that I opened myself up to at least reading some of his words for myself. What I found was, as usual, not as rumors portrayed. Everyone has their own story to tell and sometimes others choose to tarnish differing perspectives. I have not read much of his work but find wisdom and merit in:

The Book of the Law

Crowley clearly understood the power of energies. Sometimes negative energies are capable of creating positive outcomes and vice versa. Although I am not a follower of his practices, I find they appeal more to men and the masculine line of thinking. Sybil Leek represents the feminine. Everything I have studied, everything that comes together is always wrought through balance.

Balance is never easily achieved, nor can it be continually maintained. Life will always tip it. It is up to the powers of nature and the work of humanity to correct each imbalance.

As a collective, it is difficult to work together, but it can be done. As individuals, how we live and what we do for others is important for our own benefit as well as the benefit of the world, and potentially, even the universe.

Eating healthy foods that come from natural sources, caring for your living space and charging it with personal energies, avoiding consumerism and other toxic modern mentalities, as well as honoring nature and striving to harm no one in your path comes at a price. Everything in life costs something. Whether it is your time, energy, devotion, money, honour or integrity; it is up to us to decipher what is most important and what we are willing to pay. Acknowledging this is just the start.

Meditation

Imagine a guru levitating on a mountain top. This provides a great visualization. It offers a soothing ideal of what meditation can be for someone who practices the art of exploring their mind.

Now forget it.

That kind of expectation doesn't offer a modern picture, nor a realistic one.

Many Pagans refer to their beliefs as belonging to "Ye Olde Religion." Even I fancy myself some out-of-time woman. Despite this, I learned long ago that feeling out of place is a part of being human.

Christians, Druids, Muslims, Buddhists, Jews and people from all faiths and cultures all find themselves plagued with a sense of confusion and/or loneliness at some point in their life. This has been recorded in literature, memoirs, texts, all forms of storytelling. No matter how many people surround you in life, the only way to foster a sense of "self' or "belonging" is to let go of the idea that everyone has a large circle of friends and that all of those people are like-minded.

Popularity is fleeting. How adored or loved a person is by others is irrelevant. Long-lasting purpose allows stronger connections to develop. It has never been more important for a person to "Know thyself."

Meditation offers another helpful option for guidance. Unlike books or coven members, it is a journey of the sub-conscious. You become your own guide. When practiced enough, meditation also links one's spirit to greater energies. It can provide answers, direction, or even a glimpse into the spirit world.

But it takes practice and patience.

Instead of worrying over frequency, remember that each moment is a preparation. Everything we fill our days with eventually becomes the actions that drive our lives. I don't sit still well. I need movement. Action. I have to do many tasks to feel as if I have accomplished anything.

I never think I meditate enough, but meditation is not about filling a quota. That attitude leads to self-doubt, the opposite of the purpose. Find time. Whether it is five minutes a day or week, taking just a few minutes to clear the mind and explore beyond trivial thoughts and concerns will bring more control.

There is only so much a person can control in life. Gaining control over your brain is necessary to achieve any form of self-satisfaction. It also leads to greater success on your spiritual path which creates a chain of positivity.

The Exercises

Exercising the brain is as important as exercising the body and spirit. All are necessary to lead a fulfilling life.

When I first started, I wished to be like a priestess. Graceful and poised, I imagined I would unlock hidden talents and grow into a powerful cinematic figure. I'm also a kid at heart. Separating fantasy and reality became a challenge at first, but now I know better.

Place all your preconceived notions on the floor beside you. Keep them close. Sometimes they are helpful. But leave them there.

Meditation isn't about finding something new; it is about building off of who you already are. In my studies I was lucky enough to discover the term, "Rapid Thought". The words Bipolar Disorder were yet to earn a place in common vernacular. They still mean very little to me despite being diagnosed because it does not offer understanding. It is just the name, not the how or why.

Recognizing rapid thought gave me the knowledge I needed to start at the best place for me. Not all minds are alike. Each thought process is unique, though some are similar.

Figuring out your brain is the first step to true meditation.

For those of us who suffer from rapid thought and struggle to control what flies through our brains, the first exercise is simple. Slower thinkers may find it boring but it is beneficial for everyone. It is not a race or a competition. There are benefits and disadvantages to both ways of thinking and all the thought processes that fall somewhere in between.

 Sit with a pen and paper or tablet and set a timer for 1–5 mins. When ready, start the timer and tap a blank document every time your thoughts shift.

This is a simple practice to measure what kind of focus you have.

The ultimate goal is to gain enough control over yourself to clear your mind of everything for at least five minutes. This is still difficult for me. We live in a fast-paced world. Society puts more pressure on success and personal achievement than ever. Don't get discouraged if it takes months or even years to reach this goal.

From there, focus will come easier.

Clearing the mind is a precursor to guided mediation, or even focused exploration. Choosing what to think about is the next step. The "how" varies. Some people prefer to close their eyes. I feel silly lost behind my eyelids.

Night Time Meditation

The only time I close my eyes for meditation is when I do it before bed during busy periods of life. Some gurus warn against this. If control has not been mastered it can lead to falling asleep which brings about strange dreams that might open dangerous paths through the mind.

I have not experienced this. When I mediate before bed, my mind awakens with connections. I remain conscious and drift through my past, present, and future selves. Replaying past events and experiences aids me in making wiser choices. Allowing my body to relax in the present removes negative energies. It also offers healing power to combat sickness or chronic pain. Visualizing what can and will come to fruition makes it more attainable.

But be realistic.

Magic is not a cure for troubles. It is a spiritual map. Your energies are the compass. Meditation will not fix a person; it empowers individuals to find what they need to repair themselves.

Daytime Meditation

There are many practices that work. The simple act of walking through a quiet forest is a form of mediation to me. Breathing in clean air and waiting for a bird to chirp reminds me of greater purposes. Swimming to the bottom of a lake or stream and hovering over the bottom to let the current tickle my skin blocks out all negativity. It is where I feel the safest. Perching atop the branch of a tall tree with sap coated hands and pine needles in my face is also another favorite.

Walking away from the mundane and reconnecting with nature is one of the best ways to meditate, but it is not the best way to focus. When looking to find answers, or journey through a new idea, sitting in a small comfortable space is best. Facing an alter is helpful but not necessary, so long as you are mentally prepared.

The simple cross legged, palms up position works often. Close your eyes or find a spot to stare and feel your body. Don't rub your hands on yourself, but feel the blood pumping. Hear the pulse instead of letting the world drown it out. Inhale. Follow the sensation, the air passing in and through you.

Exhale and push out all negative thoughts, every doubt. Bring an image, sound, or idea to mind. Hold it. Make it real. Experience it with every sense as if it were in the room with you in this world.

Hold it as long as you can.

When you can hold it for the allotted time that feels right, you are ready to move forward and interact with said sound, image, or thought. From there, trust your instincts.

Humans have fooled themselves into believing they are not natural creatures. We have gone so far as to destroy certain natural bonds that give us intuition and higher reasoning. Our comfortable lifestyles make us forget about starvation, exposure, dehydration. Let yourself remember the people who have suffered so you can live, generations who worked tirelessly and those still in need around our world.

There is much we cannot control. The only thing a person has full power over is themselves and how they react to others, and we don't often have that. Not when the mind is untrained. Not when the body is poisoned. Not when society bickers over who has more in a land where everyone is rich compared to the whole population.

Meditate to clear the mind, and then control it. Meditate to truly know, love, and care for yourself so you can share that happiness with others.

Elemental Meditation

I am a fire sprite. I can build a fire in a windy rainstorm (if I'm feeling stubborn enough). Flame meditation is what sparks my soul. Lighting a single candle and placing it on a table, alter, or the floor in front of me assures results.

It is a simple exercise. I stare at the flame and let the light guide me. Sometimes I use it to clear away all thoughts, others it is my focus when building the energy to see inside my mind and control the thoughts. The smaller the flame, the longer I can forget everything else.

Meditating on full burning fires turns into scrying, which I will discuss in a later chapter. Water signs often find ease in meditating with their fingertips dipped in a small cup or basin. Earth elements can hold a rock or pebble. The trick with Air signs is anything from sitting in a blustery storm, to turning on a fan – not very ethereal, but if plugging in an electric device seems counterproductive, waving a hand fan is another solution.

Connecting to the energy of your element's symbol draws power. It offers a real-world representation of nature's own energies and their meaning in our lives. Everything in ritual and magic is about feeling what is right. If burning incense and chanting gives you more focus, add that. If shouting and banging a gong increases control, run with it.

Every material used is just an object designated to help bond you to the spiritual connection we all share. For some it brings us closer to the Gods or our ancestors, on occasion, both.

Finding a comfort zone and pushing it at a safe pace will drive more energy which can lend heightened abilities.

Art as Meditation

The art of creative outlets and self-expression can be spiritually empowering. Not everyone needs to sell a painting to enjoy stroking paint on the brush. Nearly half of the human population can carry a tune, at least sing well. Whether crocheting, computer programming or even writing, humanity has more access to different materials, instruments and studies in the arts.

For some it is a hobby or a way to enjoy passing time. When incorporated into rituals and spell-work, they become godly. Music and dancing are always encouraged in ritual. Drum circles and free movement are the easiest way to build energy.

My family and I always pound drums, shake maracas and tambourines while circling the alter during the Sabbats. On Samhain/Halloween we write notes to dead loved ones and send them on the air by burning them in our ritual fire. When the world seems to be falling apart and I can't read one more depressing headline, I retreat into my house in search of colors to smear on canvas. To celebrate the wonder of childhood, I crochet for new babies and my children.

All of these practices have purpose and many can be fused with hopeful energies that serve as luck charms. It is up to each person to find what sparks their interest. Explore. Take classes. Listen to others. Share stories and maybe find a new talent that's been hiding for years.

As that knack blooms, incorporate it into daily schedules, or utilize infrequency as a power surge. When it comes to meditation and personal ability, no one can dictate what is best for someone else. I can write what I know. I can share my findings. But as with most of life, it is not until a person experiences for themselves that they fully grasp what is out there.

I use the term art to define any voluntary act that brings about some end a person can share and marvel at once finished. To some, even childbirth is an art. (I've had three natural homebirths and there is definitely a skill one acquires after a few go-rounds.)

The spiritual path is a blessed one. It is not always easy, and not everyone wishes to understand it. Finding yourself is all that matters.

Self-Awareness

I am not lost, nor have I ever been. I don't believe that anyone truly is. The "finding-yourself" metaphor is too clichéd and it loses the point. The spirit is all about self-awareness. "Knowing thyself."

However we package the idea, the main goal is to be in control of your energies so you can create better changes in life. Here comes the, "life is change" cliché. I like to add to it and speak of balance. Nothing in life is permanent. In order to better cope with every change, one must constantly strive to achieve balance.

It's impossible to always attain it because life keeps shifting as we grow and learn more. Being in control is not always an option. To maximize personal satisfaction and improve focus you need to be able to trust yourself and your instincts.

But how does a person develop that sense-of-self?

Living the lifestyle that best suits you is the first step. It sounds easy but is difficult in practice. I myself wish to maintain a healthy body so I can take care of myself at all stages of life. I need a healthy mind to continue a healthy spiritual life. Utilizing this power of three (something anyone who has any idea of magic will have heard) will help.

Meditation is the start, but it is just one single aspect of becoming fully aware of what you are capable of. Everything you eat, do, and absorb affects your entire existence.

It sounds a bit overwhelming when laid out like that. Avoiding fast food, junk food, drugs, alcohol, fake news, psychic vampires, social drains and other negative influences is nearly impossible. There is not one perfect being on this planet.

Reminding myself of that helps. Perfection may be the goal but recognizing that it is a lifelong journey will ease the pressure.

I am not writing to ask anyone to be perfect. I'm the most imperfect person in the world. I am stubborn, harsh and inappropriate at times – to myself and to others. Knowing these defects helps me to work toward softening my issues and potentially chipping away at them to make sure I don't harm others with my character flaws.

I eat cake. I splurge and enjoy wine. This does not mean I cannot push myself to avoid gorging on processed sugar. It is a balancing act. Everything you eat fuels your body, changes how you think. When I eat vegetables, fruits, lean meat and nuts I am at my best. I feel good inside and out.

I do reward myself with junk once or twice a week, but if I go overboard, I find it difficult to think clearly and deal with life.

It is also important to make sure I force myself to work hard even when I don't feel like it. I write for a living. It sounds romantic and lovely, but it's grueling. No one rewards bad writing, and payouts are not guaranteed. Like any vocation, it is taxing and often times emotionally distressing at the professional level.

Giving myself a set schedule during the week helps. I wake up and drink a big glass of water, then exercise and spend time with my family at breakfast before going to work. After I put in my eight hours, I play music, laugh, read and dance with my family. Making time for friends is another task that offers many happy returns.

To balance the rig-a-ma-role I try to give myself a few unstructured hours on the weekends to just be lazy. This reminds me of being a kid. Sometimes you have to forget you're an adult and stop looking at the time, but not for too long.

It doesn't always work. I often fall short of my own expectations. Life happens. What matters is that no matter how many times we fail ourselves, we keep striving to do the things that keep up healthy and allow us to be happy. This will show in all your workings. Meditation, magic, elemental work, all of these are waiting to be explored with vigor.

Knowing when to shut off the outside world is a major influence. Taking at least one day a month to disconnect from all technology provides time for creative surges. Getting away from phones, screens and the internet society of faceless people with judgement issues encourages balance.

These things are not easy to do. If they were, everyone would do them. To be wholly committed and walk the magical path, a person must put in every effort.

At the risk of turning people away, I choose to be honest. Instead of working to sell a book that sheds few layers and sells more materialism than enlightenment, I am placing honest words here to emphasize the severity of any spiritual devotion.

As a child I sought religion. I begged my mother to take me to church. Something inside me burned to connect with a higher power. I felt bonds deeper than expression, but my mother worked a lot and my father clearly stated, "I don't bother God and he doesn't bother me."

Like many American children born in the 1980s, I was raised on boxed macaroni and cheese and Little Debby snacks. My body thickened and the only thing that kept me from becoming morbidly obese was my love of movement and the outdoors.

When I was able to get away from that lifestyle, not only did my physique reward me, but eating fresh fruits and vegetables made my brain work better. I could think clearer, focus on what really mattered instead of giving way to anxiety.

Everyone has choices to make, and every decision does matter. That can build a great amount of pressure. In our overly connected world one can lose sight of themselves and their individual purpose. Looking at the bigger picture is important when appropriate, but a sense-of-self has to come first. If you don't have confidence you will get swept away by this world.

Acknowledging mortality and the beauty of all ages is another great feat. There is only so much we can do in life. Death awaits everyone. Children, adults, teens, the elderly, all will pass on at some point.

When first addressed, that is a terrifying concept. Humans like to believe we know everything. In the west we live as though we will never die, avoiding reminders of the inevitable. When a child dies people act as if we are entitled to live forever, mourning for months and selfishly wallowing in despair.

Not so long-ago death lived alongside everyone. It remained close by, waiting to carry off the sick, injured, and weak. We are fortunate to see lowered adolescent deaths. Modern medicine has some perks (though I am also suspicious of pharmaceuticals because, like magic, they always come at a price).

Being self-aware means emerging from the dark and refusing to hide from reality. It's about listening to nature's call, realizing that our limited time is a gift. Determining to balance each day and strive toward a beneficial lifestyle not only produces a better quality of life but also improves the lives of others. If a person cares for themselves, they are better able to aid others.

Besides eating well, exercising, and living a natural life, the greatest practice a person can incorporate into their day is one for mental health. People love to *talk* about *talking* about mental health, but the conversation goes awry after that. Some people use their mental illness as an excuse or a crutch.

"Oh, I have bi-polar."

Yes, so do I. That does not give me free license to misuse others or snap at strangers. Decorum is still a rule that allows people to live in harmony.

Some cannot help it. I know well the struggles of mental breakdowns. After surviving my father's Irish temper and an abusive first love, I attempted suicide at sixteen years old. Rash decisions hold repercussions that last a lifetime.

Balance and lifestyle do not always offer the key to mental health, but they will aid you on your path. I have a phobia of pills. Maybe that is because my suicide attempt was executed with pills and alcohol. Whatever the reason, I turned down living on lithium and have spent every day since then forcing myself to seek the best life possible in order to avoid that necessity.

Everyone's journey is their own. It would never be right of me to tell others what methods work best for them. Nor has anyone's disgust at my refusal to buy into big pharma deterred me from appreciating fulfillment in a natural lifestyle.

This is why knowing yourself and following your instincts are the first steps to a magical life. Once a person knows what they are capable of, they hold more power than anyone who is still floundering.

A great deal of people are suffering from mental illness today. The spectrum for insanity has changed. It seems every psychiatrist is quick to diagnose. Maybe humans were always this way; maybe modern lifestyles are too far removed from our natural dispositions. No matter what the cause, setting aside a few minutes to talk to oneself has great healing energy.

Confidence issues and a lack of focus breed from the same place. It all comes back to your brain, the true spiritual center. I often talk to myself when alone. Each time I pass a mirror I take a moment to smile at myself, pick out at least one thing I believe is beautiful.

It is not admissible to make out with your own reflection in a gross display of egotism. That is imbalanced. Just a nod or friendly glance is all it takes.

Then at the end of the day, before meditation or sleep, talk to your loved ones or yourself. Vocalize what the worst part of the day was. Talk about it. Get it out. Don't hold your emotions in; that hinders the soul.

Once you expel the negative, speak about the best part of the day. Remember the beautiful moments, laughter, or joy. Anything that offered a sense of peace, even if only for a second, is worth giving more thought to. This will train your brain to recognize and accept the negative aspects of life while extending a bridge to cross over to greener aspects as well.

It balances the mind, therefore regulating mental issues and at least offers a healthy coping mechanism for all troubles.

The Nurture of Nature

Everything starts at home. One's body is the home of the spirit, but what about beyond that?

I was raised in rinky-dink apartments in Saint Louis County. It was not until I turned thirteen that my family moved to a house, and in my teen years apartment life was there waiting to embrace me when forced to escape the darker side of suburban life.

For a brief period I was homeless. No, I did not frequent overpasses and keep warm by garbage fires. That stereotype is not everyone's reality when they have nowhere to go. I always had a place to stay. The Gods have always gifted me with at least one friend to turn to.

In my early twenties I lived in a hotel in Los Angeles. Stuck up on the fifteenth floor of the haunted building, I never took the elevator and didn't answer the door when ghosts knocked.

I am currently a homeowner with a third of an acre to do with as I please. My husband and I are raising a family just outside of a municipality so we are not forced to abide by silly rules put in place by authorities who wish to control suburbia. We are ecstatic about growing our own food and contemplating adopting a couple of chickens to share our space with, in return for fresh eggs.

The idea of retiring to farm life intrigues me.

Throughout all of these phases, my connection to the earth remained. No matter what your living situation, anyone can stay in tune with their natural self. It strengthens energies. Beyond meditation and self-awareness is the need to find a place in the world and cultivate it.

For City Life

Concrete jungles leave little room for forests, but I have never been to a city without a park. Trees may not line every street, yet they still sprout up in urban neighborhoods. Pigeons are pests to some. I saw them as a sign of hope when I lived on Skid Row. The real one.

Downtown L.A. sometimes smelled like a toilet exploded. Smog hazed over sunshine. Rats ran along side streets and alley ways, but only on the safest nights. Hopping busses and struggling to afford a tiny hotel room does not provide the space for outdoor gardening. I know this first-hand.

Connecting with nature isn't always about wandering desolate trails and climbing mountains. If it were, humanity would be in greater trouble than it is. When I lived in the heart of a city, I had to look for the Gods. They hid in shadows and danced in weeds that sprung up between sidewalk slabs. I felt their energies only when I paid close attention.

It's difficult to focus when surrounded with bustling life. It's nearly impossible for an untrained mind saturated in this mania when technology is everywhere. Something as simple as a potted plant can serve as a guidepost.

My green thumb is yellow at best. I've killed more houseplants than a person should be able to. My sister grows things by accident. She buys fresh garlic and it multiplies until she has a kitchen full of new plants she can't keep. I love receiving her latest buds, and stick to desert plants. If you kill a desert plant, maybe rocks are better suited for your needs.

One simple houseplant is a great start. Find a sunny spot to nurture it. Garden spells work just as well on potted plants as outdoor greenery.

Bamboo is easy to acquire for cheap. Small stalks in cute ceramic dishes will only grow as big as the space they are given so they are perfect for small apartments or hotels. It also doesn't need too much direct light and is a symbol of luck. I highly recommend it.

My mother once gifted me an African desert plant that also lasted for years. It filtered the air indoors, rarely needed water, and did well even when not placed in sunbeams. I kept it alive for nearly five years. It grew strong and even reproduced, something that gave me confidence in myself and lent pride in the very dirt it came from.

When I was a baby or maybe before I was born (the timeline is unclear), my parents received a luck plant from a neighbor. I don't remember her but my mother said she had a bit of the sight (the ability to see the future). She was an odd woman who once told my mother's future and all came to pass as I grew up.

This plant was a big leafy friend. I would sit and pet its stems. They were so smooth and comforting. The energy it gave me was better than caffeine.

Whenever the leaves shriveled or the stalks withered, my parents would have trouble at work or we took a financial hit. When everything came up green, it did so in all avenues. This was not a superstition it was our life. My sister and I counted on that plant. Our parents learned to guard it.

Plants are the ultimate symbol of life. Whatever you grow should be honored as such. They are great listeners and wonderful decorations.

Rocks are also another natural vessel of nurturing. Smooth river stones bring peace. Fairy stones with holes through them remind us of our sense of wonder and hold a bit of protection in them. Even big awkward forest rocks remind a home of adventure and the comfort of having a roof to return to once the outside world tires us.

Collecting rocks thrilled me when I was a girl. I searched any wooded area for layered stones that spoke of underground treasures. Like many children, I imagined finding gold. Limestone and quartz sometimes found me and my sister, but plain pebbles in creek beds still gift me a deeper love of the world.

Decorative rocks and sea shells are not difficult to come by. The preference is always to adorn your space with something you found yourself, but perusing a shop or local seller's goods is somewhat of a quest in itself.

For those living in city houses, these principles are just as applicable, plus many city homes offer porches, decks and sometimes enough land to tend a nice garden. Decorating with life and stones gives any house charm.

When I lived in my first house, the cute little brick one story had a spacious backyard that welcomed me with trees, lush grasses and often wildlife guests. Instead of spraying for pests and hunting down raccoons and opossums, I accepted nature as it strived to belong to our constructs.

I laid down grass seed and composted. I reused torn down concrete to line my gardens, and grew shade plants looking north. A community garden gifted me the ability to grow some of my own food. Nothing tastes better than fruits and vegetables straight from the earth. No refrigeration necessary.

Check around and see about joining or starting a community garden. Cities are for people and people live happier when they commune with nature. The Sun shines on all parts of the world. It doesn't matter how small your dwelling is. It is yours and you make it your own by bringing it to life.

For Suburban Life

Aah! – suburbia. It's easy to picture. Cookie cutter houses, sidewalk lined streets, grocery stores and lots of schools.

I envied this picture as a child. Grew to resent it as a teen. Now as a mother and homeowner, I realize that each community is different. I prefer a big backyard with trees to climb. Hardwood floors are friendlier to me and easier to clean. I don't appreciate carpet like some people because it feels artificial to me. It offers too much padding. I want to feel life in each step.

I don't need too much space because I don't like "stuff." I don't want to buy "things" just because I have a house to decorate. I'd rather paint pictures, craft decorations. A fire pit is a necessity, especially if the place does not house a wood-burning fireplace. My home sits in an unincorporated space outside a municipality, so I can tear down walls or build what I want on my property.

My neighbors are friendly and diverse. We live near a retirement community and I am very protective of the old souls who drive under the speed limit.

My sister is the opposite. She lives in a big giant house with lots of carpeting and knickknacks. If she wants to do any construction on or in her home it must be approved by the city. There are numerous rules and regulations she and her family must abide by. She prefers to stay indoors like my mother, but her life is just as fulfilling as mine because she too employs her natural abilities. She crochets blankets and sews clothing. Her daughter loves music and dancing.

I'd like to point out that we do not live very far from each other. Her house is less than a half hour's walk from mine. About a five-minute drive. Our streets look very different, but they harbor the same kind of love and laughter.

A home is not defined by how many rooms or stories it has. I always judge a place by what kind of energies it gives off. Your living space grows to cater to your style, your needs. My writing desk sits in my living room because word art plays an important role in my life.

Bookshelves decorate the walls with numerous titles from every genre. Works of art created by myself and my family members are displayed in a colorful array like a warm hug waiting to embrace visitors. Musical instruments often soak the walls in melodious tunes. Yoga mats sit rolled on the basement floor ready for their morning use.

None of this is accidental.

I do not have some gold altar glowing in an eerie corner. No eye of newt or rat tails hanging from it. Altars are useful, yes, but I find the traditional use of one impractical.

Maybe I have grown too immaterial, but my coffee table serves as the perfect site for ritual offerings. It is a constant in the heart of the house where babies have pulled themselves up, tired feet have rested, and pictures have been drawn.

Full Moon rituals and the Wheel-of-the-Year do not require me to sit in front of an alter chanting all day every day. I have too much life in me for that. My meditations are often outdoors or in bed.

I prefer open windows to air conditioning and blankets to a heater. Bringing the outdoors in is something I've done since before lasting memories. Gathering sticks and twigs, rocks and leaves for ritual prepares me for spiritual communion. It also allows my house to breathe with a sense of existence in the natural world.

These priceless gifts from nature's bosom are arranged on the coffee table and transform it into a true altar in times of Pagan worship. If one is not fond of dirt and debris in the house, they can either ignore their neighbors and do all their rites outside, or they can clean everything as much as they like. Soaking rocks in buckets outside, tying sticks together to design symbols, and clipping fresh flowers from gardens are similar to ritual baths which cleanse our bodies before Sabbats.

Like cities, suburban areas do not have endless fields and rolling hills, but they too are home to countless parks. Stretching one's legs or taking a short drive leads to small community preserves or even nature reserves. Get to know your area. Look around. Find friends who appreciate you. Nurture the land and get acquainted to your specific grounds.

Get dirty. Plant a few flowers. Run through the grass barefoot – this is even better in a warm summer rain. Start a garden. Plant as many fruit trees, bushes, and vegetables as you can. Your body will reap the benefits and reward your mind.

For those who work long hours, I understand the agony of fatigue and the fear of modern pressures. They plague my life every day. There will never be enough time to fit everything into each day.

All a person needs is just one hour, or even one half-hour a week to go outside and work the land. I can tend a decent vegetable garden with just two hours a week set aside for it. Sundays are my gardening day and I make sure to spend two hours pulling weeds, digging rows, planting seeds and dropping natural fertilizer.

Fish is a great fertilizer. Planting fish with seed is an old Native American trick. Coffee grounds and rabbit poop also enrich the land. Composting green garbage (foods) and brown garbage (papers) can produce healthy fertilizer if turned well.

Leaving a corner of your garden free for the bugs and backyard critters to eat makes a great offering to the Gods. To protect crops without spreading poisons, my favorite reliable method for protecting my food as it grows is spraying hot sauce on the rest of the garden. It washes off easily enough.

Depending on the weather, the sky may be kind and offer enough rain to grow a healthy garden. I usually leave it up to the Gods, but I do not live in a desert region. Be water conscious.

If your body or lifestyle does not agree with this form of connecting with nature, rock gardens, sand gardens, or even setting out a simple bird bath will serve as a different outlet.

Age creeps up on many people. My maternal grandmother was a city girl until she got married; she did not run outside with the children as I do. She had a few little gardens, but she often looked out at her bird bath and found serenity in watching our feathered friends drink and splash in her yard.

Hanging a potted plant by the front door or just stepping out on the porch to watch the sunset nurtures our need to be one with the natural world. Yes, I still have a potted plant I continue to try and keep alive.

My most recent victim is a gardenia. I dared to care for a flowering bush. My husband gave it to me and it has lived for almost a year. This may be in part to my allowing it hours outdoors in the fresh air and sunshine. I've been careful to water it during indoor intervals but the outcome is yet to be determined. It is currently still growing, but stiff and many leaves have fallen off.

It is important to keep testing our abilities. I will never be a garden witch but that doesn't mean I can't try to grow something inside. It's a challenge, but also a trial that I need to remind myself it is okay to fail as long as I don't let negative results stop me.

It helps me slow down. Sometimes we need to pause, or stop. We get caught up in the day-to-day hassles. I do it. Everyone does. But there is a sweet solace in having your own space. Utilizing it for a deeper purpose, such as planting, leads toward the divine.

For Rural Life

I am not a farmer. Nor have I ever been. Despite this I've put in hours on a farm that includes working in fields, harvesting from a green house, caring for chickens and cows. Why? Because my dad moved away and decided to live in the country and get back to what he knew.

I did not know my father's side of the family well. He was raised on a farm. His mother had a rough exterior but a good mind on how to handle her house. When my parents got married, my dad struggled to fit in with suburban life. It made him feel suffocated. He lashed out, sometimes at her or me and my sister. Being the most outspoken of the three, I had my differences with him for some time, but once he moved onto greener pastures things evened out.

Getting away from the cities and bypassing populated areas is a truly unique experience. It's not easy for me to glimpse a view free of powerlines and streetlights, so I appreciate the opportunity to escape civilization whenever I can.

Breathing clean air relieves the mind. My cell phone loses its signal, but I prefer that out there. Getting away from the pressures of our cramped lifestyles is like going back in time. It is not for everyone, but I think we could all enjoy a day in the wilderness at least once a month.

When you're outnumbered by trees your perspective shifts. The mind grows more attentive to the little things that make life worth living. A wildflower scented breeze can erase tension. The sound of a hawk overhead calls to a primal aspect of life.

My mother's Uncle Johnny owned a farm with her Aunt June when I was a child. One of my favorite memories is going there when I was about five years old and helping Uncle Johnny out. A strong sense of purpose came with collecting eggs. Wandering the open spaces alone made me feel bigger.

I also worked as a veterinary assistant in my twenties. The clinic I served at didn't just see cats and dogs, we saw everything. My boss was a zoologist. We had reptiles and birds too, but the funniest memory was running around the neighborhood behind the clinic trying to help one of our neighboring patients catch their pet pig who had gotten loose.

I jogged up and down the sidewalk with a couple of volunteers. Unsure of how to call a pig, I held the slip-tie leash in my hand and tried grunting, oinking, and calling out, "Hello pig." It answered to my words best.

My father's farm has its moments. He treats his cows like dogs so they come running up the hill when I pull into the driveway. They push each other out of the way to get to the fence first and moo at me like children begging for candy.

They are sweet, sensitive creatures who care for their young better than a lot of people do. We hand feed them alpha cubes, but they live a free-range life eating grass from the meadows. They get rub downs, hugs, and sometimes kisses.

My dad only kills the males since they are more aggressive, which makes me shower them with more affection to give them the best life possible before they are sacrificed so we can eat. I once abstained from eating meat but have since come to allow myself only free-range meat from animals that lived well. This is the best choice for me and my lifestyle.

The chickens are fun to feed. They run around pecking at whatever they can find. They are less affectionate but love exploring. Also, the free-range birds are protected by a large roost house that is shut up at night to protect them from predators. In return, we don't eat them often. Their purpose is to provide eggs. When they get old and feeble then their fate is delivered.

I love walking the acres with my dad. Walking the forests and climbing tree stands allows me to see everything I miss back home. There is a fresh water spring that supplies a creek with water on the property and I cup my hands at it and slurp great big gulps of water as nature intended.

Not once has this ever made me ill. It is like the fountain of youth. The minerals in that water revive my senses. They cool my body in ways no purified bottled water could. It lubricates my body, my organs for any trials to come.

When I leave I do miss it.

A life of open land is my future. It will offer the freedom to host open rituals outside without fear of neighbors snooping around passing judgement. It will allow me to walk with nature every day. It will guide me through the last phase of life toward the realms that lie beyond.

I know this as sure as I know the alphabet or the order of the planets.

I encourage others to take pride in where they live, no matter which of these three areas they hail from. It will do well for you to test out all three. One does not have to live in a city, suburb, or rural land to reap their benefits. Visiting a farm opened to the public for harvest festivals or wandering a city celebration gives insight. Plenty of suburbs host events that welcome all.

We are more accepting of what we know.

Because I was raised in a suburb and then moved to a city I hold the notion that children are best raised in the middle ground suburban areas because it is easier to go to a city *and* appreciate a small town when having lived in an area that is somewhere in between, but I know plenty of city lovers and country folk who would disagree. I've adopted the idea that being born and raised in a suburb, then moving to a city for college and/ or work, then moving back to the suburbs to raise a family, and retiring on a farm are great life phases to follow.

Despite this idea, I am not blind enough to believe that what is right for me will work for others. That is why I have detailed all three experiences as separate lifestyles. No matter where I go or what I do, one thing follows me, home is a place you take with you. You are your ultimate home. The energies where you live connect with that based on how you incorporate yourself into them and that habitat.

Spiritual Lifestyle

You don't have to wander around in silk robes burning sage with crystals tied to your head to find the power within. Small lifestyle changes work best. It is easier to be consistent when the overall picture doesn't have to be redrawn.

I've known people who find Paganism, buy more incense than they will ever burn, cast sloppy spells every day, and then move onto another faith when the Gods don't show up at their doorstep. Maybe their path needed more tending, maybe it was meant to drift in another direction. There are plenty of success stories from all faiths and practices.

What assures success on any journey is care and thought. Time matters. Nothing strong can be developed in a single day or week. Allowing yourself to be patient is part of ascension.

Once a practitioner is educated with books, meditation, self-awareness and a properly nurtured home life, things wrap together in a spiritual lifestyle. It is easier to meditate when it is part of daily life. No one appreciates the earth like a person who has worked the land.

Pride will come with these accomplishments. It is expected. I am proud of my workings and encourage everyone to feel good about themselves, but discretion is a must.

There are people who will not understand. A good witch knows how to compel her audience. If you have family members who believe magic is evil and witches are devil worshippers, it's probably not a good idea to burst into their house wearing a giant pentagram painted on your head. Or if you mean to widen the divide, maybe it is.

I joke.

I would never advise anyone to closet who they are. Do not hide from your faith, but be conscious of those you are talking to. Breaking barriers comes with understanding not flamboyant displays.

I've met so many people who are amazed that I am a Wiccan. The main response is, "But you're so nice and friendly."

I laugh it off. I would rather help others realize that stereotypes have nothing to do with me and my faith. Instead of taking offense I smile.

They expect all Pagans to wear black, smoke cigarettes, and scowl at happy people. It's as silly to me as looking for someone with a long decrepit nose and pointy hat. I don't expect all Christians to picket gay weddings, nor do I think all Muslims are plotting terror attacks.

People are just people. Some of us hold the same beliefs, some of us do not. Many are just trying to live their life. I wish I could say forget about them and just "do you," but interacting with others is important and so it is also valuable to be careful when meeting new people or when adjusting your life to fit a new purpose.

Not every family member has to agree with you or your work. All you should ask is that they respect you and in return you respect their right to be confused, upset, or need time to come to terms with new knowledge. My mother read up on my faith. She found the parallels between Paganism and Christianity and supported me right away. My extended family has all their own opinions but because we're family we don't run around attacking each other during celebrations. Instead we focus on our similarities, play with the children and catch up without dragging religion into it. That is the mature thing to do. It is a challenge at times, but that is life and adulthood.

Get to know your neighbors. Become a part of your community. Volunteer, go to local government meetings, show up and be present. If you get acquainted with the people around you they will be more likely to set aside potential prejudices and educate themselves.

I worked with a conservative Christian years ago. He was very concerned about other people and openly talked about his beliefs even when not asked to. Instead of arguing with him or shouting about my faith, I ignored him. I wore a small pentacle around my neck every day. It was a luck charm and had nothing to do with him.

Our co-worker, who sat next to him, stopped to ask me about it one day. Instead of listening to his gossip about others, she came to me to find out why I wore a symbol he thought was "evil." Glad to be given this opportunity, I explained that it represents the elements coming together with the spirit to make a person whole and that even early Mormons once used pentagrams.

She said it was beautiful.

Not every exchange has been so uplifting. I dated a great guy in high school who was a true Christian. He didn't care what everyone else was, as long as they didn't hurt other people. His optimism led me to accept an invitation to go to his church and hang out with his youth group friends at a party the congregation hosted for teenagers.

I figured I would not have been invited unless it were safe. All seemed safe. Everyone was nice when introduced to me. We ate, danced and hung out and, as the night progressed, I wanted to go outside and play on the kid's playground (one is never too old to swing and slide). A small group of my boyfriend's church buddies came with. I smiled at the moonlight and the wind shifted.

"Where do you go to church?" I was asked.

My boyfriend tensed up. He held my hand and squeezed. "She's more spiritual."

"My mother used to take me to church as a girl. She's Catholic. It was nice but my church is the outdoors." I laughed.

They were not amused.

"So what do you worship?" The same boy who questioned me before asked.

"You don't have to answer that." My boyfriend stepped between us. "I invited her here, she's fine."

I rolled my eyes and stepped forward. "I believe in mother nature and the elements that bring us together."

I apparently didn't explain myself well enough. The boys and his friends sneered at me. "So, you're a devil worshipper."

"That's enough." My boyfriend glared. I shook my head and he led me away. "Sorry about them."

At the time, I was more baffled than angry at their ignorance. Many are the times I've pondered what I could have done better to represent myself and people like me in a more influential way. For a while I didn't look at Christians the same. I had met their prejudice first hand and it scared me.

Thankfully I met other wonderful open-minded Christians. I call them true Christians, the people who "judge not least they be judged." Religion can section us off into our own corners, or we can find the similarities between different faiths.

Just because a handful of Christians have been rude and closed-minded does not mean they speak for all. This principle can be applied to any group of people: races, cultures, genders, etc.

All negative experiences can be turned into useful lessons. I may not be able to empathize with people who jump to preposterous conclusions, but I can choose not to play their games. Feeling out a situation and when to open up about your faith is tricky. It's all about instinct. Trusting yourself and your perception of others is an art. It comes from self-awareness and a well – maintained relationship with your community and others.

Looking back, I would have been wise to tell the boy at that Christian gathering that my relationship with my god was none of his business. It may have provoked him. It may not have. What happened is over and I do not need to waste time and energy dwelling on it. I have tucked that memory away for protection and only brought it out here to help anyone in a similar position utilize my knowledge and potentially create a better outcome.

I was not violently removed. No one burned me at the stake. My boyfriend spoke up with me and we left. Life went on.

Part of finding spiritual peace is learning to let go. You have to teach yourself to leave the past behind you like a shadow. It will follow you, but it will not define you unless you allow it to. I prefer to set my sights on the here and now as well as the future.

Finding that perfect space between standing out and fitting in takes courage. Letting your crazy awesomeness out at the right time usually helps because we all need to feel loved by others at times. Humans are social creatures. Even when we feel different, even when we relate to animals or plants more than other people, we still harbor a desire to find someone to talk to or laugh at the world with.

Don't rush it. The right circle will find you. You just have to be looking in the right places.

Holidays

There is always something to celebrate, especially with nature-based faiths. Most religions and/or cultures host holidays that honor the seasons. Many Christian holy days are linked to the Wheel-of-the-Year. Christmas is just a few days after the winter solstice, just as Easter is often sometimes around the first day of spring.

This stems from the long history between Pagans and monotheists. When Christianity was new, the church found it easier to convert Pagans by implementing the ways of old into their celebrations. I've heard many a Christian boast about this as if it were a charitable endeavor. Maybe it was for some. But when faced with converting or being killed, it drove entire communities into hiding.

I myself prefer authenticity. I do not celebrate Christmas, not because I don't think it's a nice celebration, but simply because I am Pagan and I have my own holiday to enjoy. I don't need a watered-down version four days later. Plenty of people choose to honor both. There is no specific way to go about it.

Whether Druid, Shaman, Wiccan, Celtic or any other branch of Pagan, there are at least four main Sabbats. The first day of a new season is highly important. The energies shift. There is potential for creating bigger changes through spell-work and meditation.

Also, the mid-way point of each season offers a tunnel of reflection and sometimes stronger gateways to the afterlife. These eight holidays are not just observed by Wiccans, but they make up the basis of worship for that specific subsect of Paganism. The Wheel-of-the-Year requires devotion and persistence.

I will first go through the main layout of our ceremonies and then detail the four Sabbats before the smaller mid-season rituals. The modern age barely allows us time to praise the changing world around us. Dedicating one's self to nature and the creators that tend it can be integrated. It is not about how long the ceremony is or how many crystals you place on your altar. Some people don't even need an altar.

Worship takes many forms. If a busy life does not allow a person to get away for eight days, then focus on the four main points. The four corners of your faith. The seasons don't forget us even when we curse them.

The main point is to go outside and connect with the energies that bind us all. Acknowledging the Gods or the creators of the Earth is a ritual in itself. Eight days sounds like a lot when having been raised by convenience. Consumerism and corporatocracy have confused us into thinking we have to buy large expensive gifts in December and shower kids with candy and stuffed animals in spring.

Paganism is more than that.

Before each ritual I like to take a nature walk and gather symbols of the season to decorate the ritual area with. Since I live in a suburban area, we do the first part of each holiday inside and the second out in the backyard. I would prefer it all free from the indoors, and it works sometimes, but a person needs to feel at one with their space and that can prove difficult with cars driving by and neighbors stepping out to interrupt.

The main thing is that you are comfortable. Each holiday should feel special. Sharing it with friends or family is always an enriching experience.

Another great way to spiritually prepare is fasting. Our society puts great emphasis on the dangers of anorexia. I would never encourage a person to starve themselves as a lifestyle, but the health benefits of three to forty day fasts are astounding. From fighting cancer cells to preventing heart disease and stabilizing blood sugar, allowing your body a break from digestion leads to good health.

In the age of the obesity epidemic it troubles me that so many people write off fasting. We are gluttons for food. It's everywhere. People can't escape fast food restaurants, advertisements and conversations centered around filling our stomachs. We have become obsessed with food and with that comes many problems.

Fasting teaches self-control. It is about mind over matter, a concept necessary to be self-aware. It is linked to higher brain function and may even slow the aging process.

When choosing this option, take it easy. A one day fast should always be the first step. Test it out. Talk to a doctor or listen to your body.

I swear by the three day fast. My body feels cleaner, stronger after three full days (and nights) without food. Yes, seventy-two hours.

As I grow older it's more important to control my diet and exercise but it gets much harder each year. The seven day fast is now my goal before every ritual celebration. It makes the feast more important and enjoyable.

Ritual baths also help cleanse the body and prepare the soul. Relaxing in a soak of warm water is meditation. It centers the mind. The steam gives energy.

These methods increase personal power. Preparations should change and be modeled based on individual needs, but the foundation remains. So now that we know how to get ready, the rites are ready to be performed.

Each celebration is held the night before the solstice, equinox, or mid-season. That provides the most returns. Doing it within a few days before or after is better than none at all but try to keep it close, and nighttime is the best time for rituals because you will need rest afterward.

First we cast a circle around our alter, fire, and/or working area. My altars are never displayed the same but I do place a Gods candle and Goddesses candle beside each other at the north end. I carve their symbols in the wax. I find they are best represented with white candles which are free of any influential colors.

Then I choose a host of seasonal candles. Some holidays are better served with one, some with three or more. If burning incense or oils feels right, the best scents are ones that fit the season. Crystals are always welcome but again, stones found on your own walks are more meaningful.

Gathering a small bowl of salt and water is sometimes necessary if you wish to do spell-work or be fully protected from outside elements. The water should be charged (or blessed). It is easy to do. Either you or a ritual companion should dip their fingertips in the water and focus on feeling their energies. They should direct that power out through their hands and into the water.

When ready, get up and walk in a circle around your ritual area. If needed, sprinkle salt and water as you go while chanting your own lines about casting a circle in the name of the elements: earth, air, fire, water, for protection and invite the Gods or energies that be to join you (and your coven, family and/or friends, if not alone).

I always walk around thrice, but ritual is personal and finding your own set of standards and rules is something that comes with experience. Once cast, my husband (the male figure) lights the Gods candle. He has studied Aleister Crowley and chants to welcome Ra/The Sun/The Gods. We follow his lead until it is my turn to light the Goddesses candle and lead everyone in a chant to welcome Freya, Diana, etc./The Moon/The Goddesses.

Once done, we light the seasonal candles and sit and meditate together. If spell-work is necessary, we perform it here.

Afterwards we stand with percussion instruments. We have hand drums, a tambourine, shakers and wood blocks, one for everyone to beat together as we dance and skip around the circle. At first, we start slow, and gradually go faster and faster with the beat to build energy. This drum circle is the children's favorite part. They laugh and sometimes we make up words and sing. The point is to harness the combined forces of joy.

When we go as fast and get as loud as we can, we stop and turn to the alter candles and send that energy into the world. Sometimes it's in general, but often times if someone is sick, or suffering, we send that energy to them. This is all decided just before the drum circle starts.

After all the excitement, hunger growls and so we feast. Each Sabbath calls for different dishes, but the love is the same. We go around the circle telling each other our favorite part of the season as we enjoy foods made from scratch. I am a kitchen witch and only trust healthy natural ingredients. It is easier to appreciate a meal you worked hard to create, but any foods can be used.

Once finished, we do crafts with the kids and I read Pagan children's stories. The Rupert and the Wheel-of-the-Year books are a favorite.

Then it is time for presents. We give no more than three for each holiday and usually one big one, if that. The point of these rituals is to grow deeper bonds, not try to impress people with material items.

Our ceremonies are similar each time, but the details depend on the holiday.

Winter

The Winter Solstice is pure joy. Also known as, Yule, the first Sabbath after the Pagan New Year (Samhain), hosts many similarities to Christmas. Like the Christian holiday, evergreens are an integral part of decorations. They remind us of strength even in the darkest times.

Holly berries and mistletoe are perfect winter plants to adorn your home with. I prefer to decorate a tree outside for outdoor rituals, but my husband wishes for the quiet of our peaceful home, so we decorate out and in. Hanging live wreaths and wrapping pine garlands outside inspires smiles throughout communities without wasting energy.

The best Yule candles are red and green to mimic these winter plants. In addition, I like to carve pictures of wintery snows and strong trees on them. Your nature walk probably won't offer much more than pine cones, but other decorations are fine to place within your circle. I have a statue of a Cardinal and ornaments of other winter birds.

A Yule log should be selected before ritual. It is customary to anoint it with cinnamon and wrap it with pine, but it can be rubbed with those oils instead. It should be set on top of the center of your woodpile before lighting the blaze as it represents the light and warmth that will keep you safe in the coming months.

Spell-work for change, healing, and prosperity is best this time of year. Foods to serve include fish and venison, nuts, late harvest vegetables like broccoli and cauliflower, fruitcakes.

Spring

The Spring Equinox is also called Ostara. It is a celebration of life. This first day of spring is similar to Easter. But instead of flopping around the calendar between two different months, Ostara is at the end of March, usually on the twenty-first. Like the celebration of Easter, eggs and fluffy animals like sheep, bunnies and lambs represent the joy and hope of birth.

We decorate hard boiled eggs and charge one special one with our energies by meditating on it and pushing the warmth of our bodies out through our fingers into the chosen egg. Then we hide them all and the children who find their magic egg are granted a small wish. I always remind my children not to ask for too much, there are too many people in the world to constantly ask for mass miracles.

It is fun to weave baskets from paper to egg hunt with. The hunt is of course done at the end of ritual as the gift giving ceremony and we often exchange a couple of small gifts and maybe one larger one.

Spring candles are yellow and light green as a reminder of the warmth coming upon us. I often carve pictures of the Sun and flowers. Your nature walk might not host many wildflowers yet, but sticks and twigs should sit among the waking grasses. Hyacinthus flowers are the exception that I love in my garden. These hearty flowering plants will grow in shade and bloom in early spring, snow or rain.

If you feel a need for incense or oil, florals are best.

Spell-work for growth, hope, and rebirth is best this time of year. Foods to serve include eggs and ham, cheeses and seeds.

The morning before or after ritual is the best time to start a garden or plant new early spring seeds. Planting an eggshell from one of the ritual eggs will give your plants nourishment and protection.

Summer

Even though it is the Summer Solstice and the first day of the season, it has earned the name: Midsummer. Being a summer born baby, this is my favorite, though I love all seasons in their turn. Welcoming longer days and naps in the shade is all about savoring life. Midsummer is also a time when some believe that the fairy realm is more transparent to human eyes.

This can sometimes be chalked up to hallucinations brought on by too much heat exposure from hiking, swimming and imbibing in ritual wine (all encouraged this time of year). I've been led away from the man-made world and traipsed through a place no one remembered or could find, so I have my own romantic beliefs on the subject. It does not matter.

Chase butterflies. Catch lightning bugs. You will never be too old. If you're able, climb trees. That will get you closer to the Gods than anything else.

The candles at Midsummer should be forest green and dark yellow or gold. Carving pictures of butterflies, birds, and bugs into the wax gives them a special touch. Your nature walk will host numerous weeds, grasses, and wildflowers. Pick just a few. I always find it disheartening to kill something beautiful in its prime, but when done for ritual sacrifice it serves a greater purpose.

Incense or oil should be musky like the forests.

If casting spells, works of healing, protection, and strong relationships are most appropriate. Fruits, nuts and berry juices are perfect for the feast. As a special treat I do s'mores once a year, and on this night only.

Outdoor gifts are perfect for this holiday. Plants, seeds, gardening toys, books about nature, toys meant for wide open spaces and wooden décor all fit into the season.

Fall

"Do you remember... the twenty-first night of September?" I can't resist singing Earth, Wind and Fire when writing about Mabon, better known as the Autumn Equinox. My youngest daughter was born the day before the first day of fall, so pardon my love of disco.

I live in the middle of the U.S. just outside of my hometown of Saint

Louis, MO. Born and raised there, I've traveled a fair amount, but nothing is like the leaves at home come fall. It was my grandmother's and my mother's favorite time of year. It hosts enough beauty to enchant anyone. Your nature walk will fill baskets with acorns, crab apples, dandelions and early leaves of gold.

The candles at Midsummer should be orange and brown. I love carving images of leaves and swirling wind onto their wax.

Incense or oil should be airy like nutmeg or apple.

Balance spells and divinations work best on Mabon. My tarot cards are always "chattier" between this holiday and Yule.

The feast for this ritual is a harvest celebration. Corn, apples, nut breads and poultry are the best ingredients to serve however you like. Corn plays a large role in the smaller mid-season celebration of Lammas on August 1st. That first harvest is a time to make corn dolls. If you read ahead and choose to create little dolls out of corn husks, Mabon is the time to burn them for luck. They are a symbol of change and letting go, making something from the earth and then giving it back when it begins to rot.

As usual two to three gifts are plenty. Nature oriented ones are always best.

Midwinter

The middle of winter can drag on. The long nights sometimes seem endless. But halfway through comes February second to shed a little light. No, I'm not talking about rodents looking for their shadows. Groundhog Day is okay but we Pagans celebrate Imbolc. It is our festival of lights. It's the night where we light a candle in each room and leave it to burn to remember the Sun and the coming summer.

Set white taper candles before ritual and walk through each room with your ritual partners (family and/or friends). Light them one by one and welcome the Gods and the spirit of the Sun back to your home. Once done, it is time to go to your ritual area and begin the rite.

Instead of singing and dancing, this ceremony is more sober. It's a time to rededicate yourself to your craft and remember that how you behave when things are at their coldest is what defines you as a person. It's easy to smile in the sunshine, but can you dance in the frost?

Meditate on that. Challenge yourself to enjoy all seasons, and be happy even when your vitamin D is low.

The candles at Midwinter should be white and red. I love to carve snowflakes into them. Depending on your area, it may be more difficult to take a nature walk before hand, but even just a few minutes outside will pinken your cheeks and, maybe, allow a few snowflakes or broken branches to find you.

Incense or oil should be crisp like vanilla.

Unlike other Sabbats, this one is about looking inward. Testing past-life re-callings or scrying to see the future is most successful this time of year. These spells are not to be taken lightly and require much nourishment afterwards. The feast of vegetables, beefs, breads, cakes and cheeses is to be set.

My family does not give gifts on the midway holidays but that is up to each host and their guests.

Mid Spring

Unlike Midwinter, the middle of spring is bursting with life. It is what most of us think of when we imagine spring. Flowers blooming, animals raising a new generation, trees green with life, everything breathes deeper. It's no wonder this time of year is all about fertility.

The Pagan name for this May first celebration is: Beltane. It's a time to pick flowers and leave them on doorsteps for friends and neighbors. Nature walks become common again. Birds sing and the air is tinted with sweet fragrances. Bringing a potted plant to the center of your rite gives a majestic focal point for meditation.

The candles at Beltane should be baby blue and dark green. Images of flowers and babies are perfect for carving into the wax. Rich incense or oils of carnation, hyacinth or gardenias can heighten your ritual experience. Handmade soaps, lotions and oils are perfect for this time of year.

When the time for spells comes, cast for creativity, growth or fertility if needed. Dairies like cheese and ice creams are an integral part of this celebration as well as buttery cakes like the Saint Louis famous Gooey Butter Cake.

No gifts are needed to enjoy this day but what spring has brought. My children and I usually make flower wreaths and necklaces for our craft time, and continue well after the celebration has ended. May poles and leaping over small ritual fires are also traditional practices to welcome this hearty time of year.

The First Harvest

There is a holiday in August – if you're Pagan. Welcomed as the first harvest, August first is a celebration of thanks. It is a time to reap what you have literally sown. Whether cultivating a farm, a backyard vegetable garden, or just a little potted herb garden, there is nothing like tasting the fruits of your labors.

This Sabbath, named Lammas, is honored with wheat, corn, and other grains. Remember the corn husk dolls I briefly mentioned in the Mabon section? You fashion those on this day either before ritual when shucking corn husks, or for crafting during ritual.

Lammas candles should be orange and yellow. Carving pictures of the plants from your garden or your favorite grain dishes adds a special touch. Any incense or oils best to burn are yeasty ones like garlic or even apple cider vinegar.

Spells for a good fall harvest, fertility and divinity will prove most successful. Before the feast, break bread and rub grains together in your hands over a plate to let the crumbs mix together. Set these aside to plant in your garden. All grains are welcome to this feast, as are fruits, vegetables, cider and wine. Sweet breads are most appropriate for desserts.

Samhain

One of the most infamous and important Pagan holidays, it dons many names. October thirty-first is Samhain to us but, Halloween, All-Hollows-Eve, the Dios De Lez Moretz and All Saints Day are held around this fabled time of year. The end of the old New Year, this time frame is one of mysticism and connections. It is known to be a bridge between the living and the dead because the realm(s) of the afterlife drift closer to us.

Some people give imagery with the popular term, "the veil thins." However you come to terms with it, the living and the dead are never closer than on Samhain.

We carve pumpkins and leave them out as lanterns to guide familiar spirits before the celebration. Alongside the leaves, acorns, rocks and other natural decorations you have borrowed from the great outdoors, your ritual space should also be adorned with memorabilia of loved ones who have passed on. Gifts, items left to you, pictures, notes, books, anything they treasured that links you to them should be included.

When it is craft time in our ritual, we write letters to those we miss and then burn them in a fire in the backyard to let the words catch wind and find their way. Burying apples for the dead is another common practice, as is going around and telling stories that make you laugh and smile when recalling the departed.

This is not meant to be a time of mourning. All will join the dead someday. Coming together to laugh and smile at our lives and look forward to what is to be is the point of this Sabbath.

Samhain candles should be orange and black. I love to carve little pictures of jack-o-lanterns and spirits on the wax. The best incense or oils to burn are allspice and pumpkin.

Séances and spell-work to see past lives or scrying into the future work best this time of year and your tarot cards will never be more honest. A feast of squash, pumpkin dishes, fish or pheasant, nuts, seeds, fruits and vegetables recently harvested, are all welcome.

Because Halloween is such a fun time of year, we watch spooky cartoons and take the kids trick-or-treating before ritual and then do our ceremony well into the night, which is more effective. Some candy is allowed afterwards for dessert, but once we've all shared our fill, we box up the rest and send it to soldiers overseas so they can hand it out to children in foreign countries.

Candy trade-ins are hosted across the U.S. and are very popular. Sometimes it is donated to shelters or impoverished areas. Giving to others remains a top goal for me, no matter where I am financially.

These holidays hold their own meaning. How they translate to you and your life is what matters. Add you own personal touches. Don't be afraid to deviate. As long as your heart is in it, the magic will be real.

The Moon

Before cell-phones, computers and calendars, we followed the Moon cycle. She shined her light on our monthly progress. We looked to the sky for guidance.

Despite modern technology, that connection still exists. Humanity continues to gaze at the Moon. There is still magic in her light, wonder in the effects she has on us. The Moon holds hope for many. Like the stars, she lends us a magical glow that can empower.

Both men and women can feel this influence, but women are more connected to this satellite. A great many Pagans look to the Moon to represent women or the female perspective just as the Sun symbolizes men and masculinity. This is due in part to our natural cycles.

Women's Connection

The Moon sways our emotions. Our bodies wax and wane with her. We grow and mature, then are most fertile at our prime. We ripen and attract our counterparts.

This is not just during life stages, but also monthly. When left to our natural state, most women are at the height of their cycle on the full moon. The weeks preceding this are harder on us, filled with cramping and loss if no conception is attempted or achieved. Once the inner lining in our bodies grows thin and disappears, we wax once more, happier, born anew.

Women are social creatures who used to share these experiences. Our cycles sync up for many purposes. The main reasons being, it allows generations to grow up together and gives women empathy to support one another, which strengthens towns and communities. We survive better; thrive longer when our reproductive cycles coincide.

In today's age, many women mask their natural connection with other females and the Moon by taking oral contraceptives. The birth control pill has its merits. I was sold on it in my late teens because my cycle is not regular, according to our calendar. Sometimes I experience it twice a month.

I was sold on the pill as a way to regulate my body. It was not until I stopped taking it to conceive my first child that I realized the negative effects. My eyesight improved, my sex drive went up, and I found it easier to connect with the Gods.

My path veered away from all pharmaceuticals at that time and I have continued to maintain a stronger relationship with my body, energies and nature. It takes more restraint and self-control to be intimate with my husband and prevent unwanted pregnancy. Coming of age in the nineties, I was taught that natural methods didn't work. Rhythms and pulling-out were all listed as ineffective no-nos.

It is true that they are not one-hundred-percent effective, but neither are condoms, the pill, or any other manufactured means. In actuality, I found breastfeeding to be more reliable than any other method, as it stopped my cycle from returning until my children were weaned. As ever, it's good to have back up plans and after having three children I am more careful than ever, but I often wonder if corporations push us to distrust natural methods to capitalize off of us. Paying to not get pregnant is a major industry, and the world is overpopulated. We're constantly being reminded of that, so we pay because it's easier than tracking your body and working with your partner.

But is easier better?

Since I have been off of the pill, I have had less mood swings and know myself better than ever. I can tell when I'm ovulating. If this does not work for you, non-hormonal means like condoms should be preferred.

Our hormones drive us to be who we are. If you mess with that, it affects every aspect of your being. I've been off the pill for ten years and am in more control of myself than ever. This makes it easier to make better decisions and be sensitive to others.

Full Moon Energy

Man or woman, the Moon gives us more enlightenment through its phases. Energy increases when the Moon is waxing. Spell-work that encourages new hopes to grow or labors to be fruitful, are more successful. This is the time to bring things into your life. It is a time to cultivate, nurture and seek new endeavors.

The full moon brings this increase in personal power to a climax. Full moon rituals are potent work. I tend to keep these rites simple. It inspires creativity. Before the full moon, I collect leftover food in a container to give back to the earth. It is a meager offering, but the sacrifice builds a link to the past. It reminds us of times when people once starved in winters and suffered heat stroke in summer.

Then for ritual, we set the altar candles as we do for the Sabbats. One white candle represents the Goddesses, or female aspect of being, and another is set to maintain the balance for the Gods, or male purpose. Not much is needed to honor the Moon in all her glory. Just set the altar in her light, preferably facing her beams.

As instructed before, make up your own chants to share with whoever celebrates with you (or for yourself, if you are a solitary practitioner). Meditations and spells will be exceptionally powerful, so take care and be specific in your workings. Scrying or reading tarot produces accurate readings on the full moon.

You may grow light-headed. Trust yourself. Out-of-body experiences are best done during this rush of power. Your subconscious will guide you as long as you maintain focus.

When mastered, a knowledgeable spirit can glance into the Summerlands, or the afterlife. Take it slow though. We are not meant to take long field-trips in unknown existences. Practice grounding after ritual to keep your mind and body connected. It is easy to get taken up in spirit. Returning to your natural state may be harsh. Coming down does not have to be like falling.

Find ways to reconnect with the material world to keep from drifting too far. Laying with limbs outstretched and breathing deep is a popular grounding technique. I like to stand on my head. Engaging in sexual activity also works well. Whatever reminds you of your physical self and its importance will do.

As opposed to the waxing/full moon potential, the waning days and nights may feel slower, maybe even depressing. They are not meant to discourage. Instead, it is nature's way of forcing us to slow down and take it easy.

We often fight this and find ourselves lashing out. Respect the process. Open yourself up to accepting that you cannot do everything you want all the time. Work schedules, family obligations, volunteer issues or conflicts with friends will happen, but waning moon magic is all about letting go. Instead of nurturing and asking to bring things into our lives, it is best to expel bad habits or ask for protection from negative influences during this time.

When you adhere to the Moon's knowledge, it is possible to reach new heights. Nature is our direct link to the Gods. Taking the time to listen to the Moon and perform rituals and spells accordingly will help your practices be more effective.

Connecting with nature and understanding the Moon helps people to live better lives. It allows us to be more conscious of the world, just as following the Sun aids people in drawing on the elements. Following the Moon's cycle helps us to have a better grasp on reality before we experiment with its boundaries.

The Sun

Like the Moon, the Sun can influence our moods and guide us. Just thinking about sunshine makes me feel warmer. I was born in the heat of summer and love hundred-degree hot sticky weather.

A true daughter of nature, I appreciate all seasons. Jumping into leaf piles in autumn, sledding in the snow, and gardening in spring are things I look forward to every year, but summer is my favorite. I love to hike and swim when the air is a thick sauna. Cooking outdoors on an open flame and marveling at lightning bugs remind me why I enjoy life.

Someone once asked me: What motivates you?

A typical interview question, I was expected to answer with a list of goals or ambitions. I *am* driven to finish what I start and connect with others, but that was not my answer. Instead I comfortably answered, "The Sun."

Upon elaboration, I explained how I love getting up early to face a new day. I never feel like I've done enough. There is always a new adventure waiting, more work to tackle (I landed that job – a full-time writing position).

Acknowledging that warmth, that spirit that comes from our life-source, wins people over. It makes you glow from the inside out. Before clocks and watches, the Sun rolled across our skies. A perfect timepiece, it subtly reminds us to keep going.

The Sun represents most of the physical attributes of masculinity: strength, persistence, leadership. These are not exclusive traits of men, but are required for males to be most successful. As the softer light of the Moon radiates femininity, the Sun burns its harsh fires upon our Earth at times like a father, like the Gods.

This heat benefits all, like the enlightening power of the Goddess moon. It can guide us toward wisdom and connect us to all four earthly elements.

Men's Magic

Men connect more with the Sun. Even in times of gender equality movements, men still hold the most dangerous job positions. These often require physical labor, often done outdoors.

My father works in construction. He has all my life. Some people think hard labor jobs are beneath them or that they are worked by people who can't find better situations. My dad loves being outside. He takes pride in seeing progress; scalable, measurable progress comes from his hands every day. We've had our own complicated relationship through the years but as I accepted the necessity for male masculinity and respect it as a natural element required to bring balance to the word, we share a deeper bond.

My husband looks to the Sun for guidance. He chants to it as the symbol of the Gods. It offers him the same connection and personal power that the Moon does for me. The Sun guides his meditations, spell-work and lifestyle.

Spring and autumn give him an energy boost that sets him on new tasks. He finds his purposes revealed at these times, where the Sun shares equal spans with the Moon, and offers enough warmth to grow thoughts and plants, forests of possibilities.

In winter he grows tired. The lack of vitamin D leaves him living like a bear hungry for hibernation. The short bursts of sunlight keep him going. He stores up his energy, his ideas, his intuition, and holds it closer.

During summer, his powers of mind-over-matter are strongest. He is from up north so he sometimes pushes himself too far and succumbs to the effects of extreme heat, but that is to be expected when we overexert ourselves.

My son was born in spring and is a woodsman already. He rarely fusses, but when cranky, a simple step outside calms him. He marvels at the Sun. He plays in its rays. His strength is increased by day.

The Sun gifts men endurance, might and agility. They absorb its power, increase their own, and funnel those energies into tasks more common for men. Yes, women can be strong and do some men's work, but that does not change certain roles.

Consistency

No matter how feminine, masculine, or non-conforming you are, the Sun is a constant in our lives. Our planet's relationship with the Sun drives our seasons and thus our connection with nature. No matter how difficult life can be, the Sun rises. Even in our darkest hours, it graces us with its magic.

That may sound cheesy – I sometimes sound like a crazy inspirational cat poster – but that doesn't make it any less true. We need constants to thrive. No matter how much I love adventure and exploration, I need something to come back to. The Sun provides that.

The Sun is our stability. Like a father, it represents structure and discipline. We must follow its example and learn to utilize its light in our everyday purposes, as well as our magical workings.

Sun magic is everywhere. Men grasp it easier but women can benefit from it as well. Spells cast under the warmest rays at the right time can hold endless force. Meditations held outside are sacred. They lift us higher if we can escape man-made noises and air pollution even for just a few moments.

It is important to also love all seasons for their importance. Winter chills our bones, but it lets the stars shine brighter. And let's not forget about snow. Snow magic leaves behind candles and material nonsense. All you need is your hands. Letting one's self really *feel* the cold and adore the marvels of frozen precipitation recalls the inner child and draws it forth to inspire new perspectives.

In spring, the rains quench not just the land but our spirit. Storms hold unsurmountable power. They can bring revelations. When meditating or casting during these peak periods, the Gods are stronger within us.

During calm periods, walking with the flowers and growing new ties to the land pushes away anxiety.

Summer heat waves are best spent soaking in a lake or stream. It's important to sweat. It expels negatives from our glands. Then the cleansing waters of the land revive the body. Freshly squeezed citrus drinks and shade have aided humanity through the worst of it for ages.

Chasing leaves, and standing through autumn breezes during harvest periods, birth healthy appetites and their rewards. None of these seasons could exist without the Sun. Everything we have, everything we are, comes from that great warmth.

Instead of finding fault with each season, choosing to embrace its turn and dance with it happily produces an outlook that extends your abilities.

Life Celebrations
(Weddings, Babies and Death)

Life is full of celebrations. Birthdays, anniversaries and other milestones are marked regardless of your apprehensions or enjoyment. I prefer to embrace every new phase. Welcoming growth and change, creates a lighter air. It offers more grace and fun.

Pagans, like everyone else, know how to party. We love to eat birthday cake just like everyone else too (although I hate icing – too sweet). This mystical idea that we have to float one inch off the ground, mumbling curses under frizzy mops of grey, or white, hair is one hell of a romanticization.

I've spent most of my life breaking stereotypes while also celebrating a unique faith that *is* different, depending on your lifestyle and calling. No matter how you light your candles or arrange your presents, we all share some similarities. The main ceremonies matter, but what about the once-in-a-lifetimes events? Marriage, births and funerals are not every day occasions, nor do they always come when we expect, but these three rites are highly sacred to us.

The details shift for personalization. Instead of having some old priest tell us our vows, most witches and Pagans write their own. Instead of washing away sin, or removing sensitive areas of a baby's reproductive organs, we ask the Gods for their guidance. When a loved one leaves us, we honor their life instead of mourning their loss.

The ideas remain constant, but these sacred rites are very personal and important to us.

Handfasting

Marriage is a heavy word. It comes with many expectations and responsibilities. I came from two parents who were never good together. My sister and I grew up begging them to get divorced, when it finally happened, they were so much better off and so were we.

For a time, I swore I'd never get married, mainly because I didn't want to ever get divorced or allow someone to have any power over me. I wrote it all off. My faith in love waned. I'm in love with love, so it was impossible to avoid. My open-hearted nature draws people in. After years of a long relationship, marriage didn't seem so scary.

Neither did divorce when I realized that finding love isn't the goal; finding someone who loves at the same level you do is what makes a relationship last. The Gods have taught me many lessons, but that one is the truest. When I found my true love we couldn't avoid each other.

His spiritual nature led us to a handfasting, something I thought I had experienced in my first wedding, but this time it was stronger, real. We walked outside in pink and black. The traditional white garb never suited me.

The leaves fell on our heads as we shared handwritten vows and acknowledged both the male and female aspects of the Gods. We included symbols of the elements and music that may as well have been written specifically for us.

Handfastings are all about binding your spirits. Most do not extend until death. It is customary to renew those vows every five years. Five years seems to be the longest time frame a person can go without changing very much. These renewals are important and strengthen relationships. By giving yourself that time frame, you feel safer, more options lay before you.

Some Pagans choose to exclude the state. Marriage licenses are not necessary to perform a handfasting, but they are if you wish for it to be a legally recognized ceremony.

Celebrating outside is always preferred. Even rain can make a beautiful entrance. Finding an officiant is easier than ever. Thanks to online certificates, your best friends can perform the rite and be recognized as state-approved, or a simple web search will bring up spiritual officiants.

What you wear and how you decorate should always be tailored to you and your partner. Succumbing to social conventions or bending to the will of a parent or future parent does nothing for you and your future spouse. Be kind, but let your day be yours.

I always wanted to wear the pink dress that Lisa donned at the end of "Coming to America." I thought it was the most beautiful dress ever made. As a child, my favorite colors were hot pink and black. When my husband expressed that those were his as well, we ran with it. His black suit and my pink dress became best friends.

We prefer smaller more intimate settings, so it was a small event, but we made sure to include the elements to remind us of our earthly connection to the Gods. Candles are the easiest representation of wind and fire. We drank wine for water, and experienced the earth by having our "flower girl" collect and drop leaves instead of killing flowers to pluck petals.

Every year on our anniversary we light the candles (pink and black, of course) and reprise our adorations. We also go through the original handfasting pictures. My husband would like to renew our vows again soon. Life is never perfect for us. We definitely have our struggles, but our connection is one we tend and nurture. I'd marry him every day if I could.

Baby's Blessing

I love kids. Maybe it's because my inner child often springs outward. It could also be because I grew up with a bunch of baby cousins and remained close with a couple of friends who became mothers in high school. No matter the reason.

Despite this, for a time I refused to consider motherhood an option for me. Like marriage, I looked at my parents and decided that wasn't for me. I feared screwing a kid up worse than I was. Now that I am the mother of three, I realize how juvenile that stance was.

Choosing to not have children based on what others have done to you just means you have not yet healed. It is the difference between being a victim and a survivor. After suffering, a person loses control of themselves or their emotions for a time. In order to move forward, they must accept what happened but regain control of themselves. The only two things we can control in life are our actions and reactions, and we can't always even do that.

Not everyone was made for parenting. Some people know this and enforce it with good will. That was not my scenario. I was merely afraid. Instead of allowing that fear to control me, I grew and listened to myself. The Gods directed me where I needed to be and I was gifted with new discoveries in meeting my children.

Each kid is different. No matter how you raise them, they come out with their own little personalities. I'm always eager to find out what they love most in life and offer my love, support and encouragement.

The first step in this is hosting a blessing. Not unlike the fairies in Sleeping Beauty, this ritual calls for gifts to be bestowed. Not packaged presents, but hopes for good health, prosperity, strength, beauty, intelligence, good humor, etc. It's tempting to ask the Gods for everything. What mother wouldn't list every positive trait?

A well-educated Pagan mother.

When performing a Celebration of Birth, you only get three. Anyone can ask for more, but the more you stretch the energies, the less likely any of them are to take hold. Never ask for too much. It's sabotage.

This celebration should be simple but fun. Invite close family and maybe a few friends as if it were a Christening, so long as all participants are understanding of your faith. It should be held on the first full moon after the baby's birth, but if that is not possible, the second is important.

Set the altar with the Goddesses and Gods candles. Also adorn it with little items that are connected to the baby: booties, handmade toys, or blankets. Then choose three traits you wish for your child. Unlike most other spells, do NOT be too specific. Asking for a child to never experience gingivitis might not be the best use of your power.

Before the ceremony, pick out three candles that will represent these traits and try to match the colors accordingly. If you wish for a happy child, yellow is a sunny smiling color, for beauty, pink often works. White is my favorite all-purpose, which you can carve little images into and meditate on beforehand.

When it is time, cast a circle if you feel the need and welcome your guests and the Gods as you light the Gods' candles. Hold the baby up to the altar and chant about the gifts you have chosen, and hold up each candle. Then light them individually, chanting, praying or singing its purpose. You may wish to gently bring the candle over the child's head, but be careful. There is no need to spill hot wax on an infant or anything like that.

Once done, siblings or the other parent can ring bells and/or a drum circle will build up the energies in the room and prepare the baby for a childhood of Sabbats. Leave the candles to burn out and feast on lots of fruits, vegetables, nuts and lean meats. Breastfeeding mothers will need and appreciate this. I know I did.

Honoring the Dead

Death comes for everyone. It is a natural part of life. We're all on loan.

This used to be a more accepted aspect of humanity. I don't know when or how people in the U.S. and other parts of the "west" became so sensitive to it. Many pretend it doesn't exist. They live as if they'll never die and avoid acknowledging the inevitable as much as possible.

I'm the opposite.

Maybe it's the Pagan in me, but I'm the person who laughs at funerals. I don't see the point in allowing someone else's death to ruin my life. Yes, some losses are harder than others. Mourning takes time, but it does not have to take shape in the form of depression.

I would never wish for any of my loved one to shut themselves off from others and fall into disarray after I'm gone. Instead of performing funeral rites or hosting a wake, I take the Pagan route. I prefer to celebrate the life and legacy left behind.

I've already forbidden my loved ones from wearing all black to my memorial. To truly honor the dead, one must live. Breathe your life in and appreciate the time you have left because that clock is always ticking.

A celebration of life ceremony should be much like a big party with a few elements from the Baby's Blessing. Decorate an alter with items that represent the spirit of the person who has passed on. Pictures and favorite clothing items are perfect. Play their favorite songs. I would like some of my silly Youtube videos shown so people are forced to laugh despite the pain they may feel. Laughter has always been my release. It keeps people alive. It bonds us and reminds us of the better times. I never want that to die.

Hosting it on the full moon or new moon is best but not always possible. What matters most is that people come together to celebrate the love they shared for the deceased. A group meditation where everyone focuses together may allow a feeling of peace, connection, or even gift some with the ability to feel the spirit if the time is right.

Food and drink are very important for this ritual. Some appetites may need aid. A lot of people forget to eat when feeling the absence of a dear friend or loved one. To combat this, have everyone bring a dish and share it openly.

I want a death cake served and maybe a mime and a juggler to perform. Morbid or not, remembering to keep death in your thoughts lightens the blow. It comes to mind often. Maybe it's because so many people I have known have died.

When I was in sixth grade, a couple who were close with our family had a baby with a heart condition. He did not live very long and that impacted me greatly. Two years later, a younger friend of mine was murdered along with his family, including his two year old baby brother. Not soon after my grandpa died.

The contrast of those two situations guided me through every funeral I attended. I've known people who died in vehicle accidents and one who was shot in the head. I did not grow up in the best neighborhood, but it was not nearly as bad as one would think, given these untimely ends.

The ones that I have trouble reconciling are suicides. I once survived a suicide attempt so one would assume that I would hold some insight and compassion for people who end their own life.

On the contrary, I have come to despise how selfish and stupid I was during my attempt. No amount of abuse or pain justifies such actions. It is something I struggle to tame when experiencing suicide second hand. I have very little sympathy for people who abandon their loved ones. It's another fault, I'm sure, but I tend to back away and leave everyone else to grieve so I don't dig deeper wounds with my harsh perspective.

Death can leave an emptiness in those who remain. To help ease the transition to living without someone, Honoring the Dead is a celebration that reminds us we are still alive and we should not feel guilty or alone in that. We all miss someone. We will all be missed by someone. That gives me comfort.

No matter who we are – no matter how rich or poor, young or old – everyone, every single person who has ever lived, has died or will die. That's a beautiful truth. We all come and we all go. That makes us equal.

Emotional Acceptance

Faith is strange. We feel it strongest when we're surrounded by like-minded individuals. Religion sprung from this connected experience. Books of rules and life lessons can offer the kind of guidance many people need. The history of theology and its necessity is fascinating to me.

I love reading about other religions. Finding similarities between other faiths and mine makes me feel as if humanity is not as much of a blight on the earth as the media often portrays. Finding the right path does not mean condemning other people. I've found meaningful friendships with monotheists, Pagans and atheists alike.

Within every group there will always be that select few, those assholes who make everyone look bad. I've dealt with plenty of "witches" who are just in it for the fashion and the spells just as I've had to avoid certain atheists who abhor anyone who adheres to any faith. There are groups within groups, subsects, because at our core we are all individuals. Every one of us has some unique thought or trait.

In order to feel loved and accepted, we often seek out approval from others. It is part of the human condition. It took me plenty of time to realize that everyone feels alone sometimes. We all hit a point where we think we are the outsider that no one relates to.

When you look past the groupthink appeal of your faith, you find the real connection. Not every Christian is anti-gay marriage. Not every Muslim believes other religions are the enemy. Plenty of atheists admit that there could be the possibility of an afterlife and even a creator, they just don't count on it.

Pagans and witches are as unique as everyone else. Sometimes we host the same kinds of rituals and celebrate nature, but we don't all have to dress or act the same. A wise friend of mine once asked me, "How do you know the difference between a new Pagan and one who has practiced for a while?"

I laughed at her smirk and asked, "How?"

She said "The new ones all dress like something out of a movie."

We were at the St. Louis Pagan Picnic and enjoyed people-watching. It was a silly observation with a hint of a joke in there. No, I don't believe that every new Pagan thinks they have to wear black capes and smocks over everything, but a great majority of the newbies do.

I leave them to it. They're finding themselves. If they feel the need to run around screaming "I'm a witch!" to everyone, that's up to them. Eventually that desire wears off and you grow more comfortable just being a person again.

This tends to be mainly common in non-blood Pagans. Children reared in the faith are more comfortable with themselves. My children are being raised to understand that we are different, we are a minority, but that does not mean we are alone or that we should look at the majority with disdain just because they follow a different calling.

By contrast, Pagans who are drawn to the faith later in life (often during their teens and twenties) find their way a bit more overgrown. The Pagan community is very accepting. They offer support and friendship. Many within it are quick to welcome anyone who wishes to seek knowledge of our ways.

This kind of love and acceptance offers an emotional support that seems to be lacking in their lives. It's one of the reasons why a good amount of LGBTQ individuals turn to Paganism (well, that and our lack of hatred against same sex acts).

To master magic and its way's a person must also learn to trust in themselves. This philosophy is not taught as broadly in other religions. People who are seeking emotional support find it in the craft because instead of looking to a savior or a prophet, we are taught to save ourselves.

I am not here to deny or confirm the existence of other religious figures. I believe Jesus was a real person. I know that the Book of Exodus had to have come from somewhere. There is truth in all faiths.

What I'm talking about is the magic within. When you realize that you can be your own savior, the monotheist teachings become less defined. They represent metaphors instead of literal tales. Maybe Jesus truly did die for our sins, but aren't we all the sons and daughters of the Gods?

It is okay to ask these questions. Even if you are Christian, or Pastafarian, asking questions allows a person to explore their faith and their link to others.

When traipsing toward the Gods, inner strength increases. This energy provides aid when questioned. It also lends patience when challenged by ignorance. I used to get upset about the "evil witch" troupe in stories and other forms of media. Over time, that anger shifted to a passion for education.

When it was suggested to me that I write about my experiences, I never dreamed it would become a writing career. Writing holds a special kind of magic. It's difficult for me to master, since I am dyslexic as well, but the human brain is a wondrous mechanism. Anyone can train themselves to learn better if they work hard enough.

Instead of focusing on the negatives in life, I choose to look at the positives and run with them. I started a book that praises the good witches in storytelling. The Glendas and Sabrinas. This manuscript has gathered enough dust to make me question it's place in the world. Some works get published, and others are for yourself.

I'm not sure if this one will ever grace the public, what matters is that it helped me look past my pain and accept that, no matter how I glare at history, I cannot change it. The future is what holds promise. Utilizing today to influence tomorrow is what brings true emotional acceptance; embracing the past and moving forward.

I suggest that everyone should possess a diary. Not everything needs to be published or shared. Some writing is more personal. It is sacred.

Writing about your journeys will help guide the way. Foreshadowing is one of the main elements of good writing. When turning the pages backward and revisiting what I've been through, I've found that my life was prepping me for what came next. It was laid out perfectly clearly, only I didn't see it.

Recognizing those patterns matters. Humans go through cycles. We turn and come back to the things that matter. Sometimes we return to bad situations due to habit or addiction. When writing it out, a person can better gauge how they should proceed.

Those conclusions educate. They turn experiences into knowledge, and knowledge into wisdom. Once you are comfortable with yourself, you can be comfortable with anyone else. Then you can take on all the rest.

Instead of celebrating Christian holidays just because everyone else does, my family and I chose to observe just the Wheel-of-the-Year, but I know plenty of Pagans who combine Yule and Christmas as one big three day festival. Some still pretend that Santa Claus exists. I once worked for a Jewish veterinarian who decorated a Chanukah tree. It's not anyone else's place to decide your religious fate.

Creating your own traditions, or incorporating others ideas into them, is a right that everyone should exercise. I struggle at Christmastime because I find the cultural holiday of consumerism grotesque. Instead of celebrating the reason for the day, many people seem to be praying to the God of shopping. The devout followers who host small celebrations and even include a birthday cake for Jesus make more sense to me.

It's difficult when dealing with family who don't understand. Some people just can't fathom walking away from a common tradition. Respecting their concerns and agreeing to disagree is best when facing those kinds of divides.

Maintaining a balance between celebrating your individuality, while participating as a productive member of society, is the best way to bridge gaps. Be an example. There is always room for improvement but if you live a happy full life and spread love and kindness wherever you go, the naysayers will get drowned out by your light.

Best of all it will draw people to you. Your energies will call on others. I first walked the Saint Louis Pagan Picnic for fun. Then I became an author who meets with readers. I never tire of talking to other Pagans, or anyone who comes to say hi. The more I write, the more fans contact me for advice. I will continue to reach out as long as people respond to my work.

This confidence was built, not born in me. Getting published in Circle Magazine before it shut down gave me a boost. I also got to hug Selena Fox years later (if you don't know who she is, look her up – she's amazing). I've traveled to Pagan Pride Day in Kansas City and Chicago. These events help connect us.

Spreading that love and helping others gain the courage they need to be who they are is what it's all about. Once you begin to come into your own, you'll find it's more rewarding to help others who struggle.

Connect

I love modern times. Technology freaks me out a little. I wonder what A.I. and robotics will bring, but for now modern conveniences have gifted witches and Pagans with stronger means of communicating than ever.

Sure, I'm a bit concerned about the dangers of being too connected and 5G. At times the tin foil hat trick sounds appealing, but in reality, society's extended ability to reach out to others has the power to spread positive energy in ways recorded history has not experienced. Modern witches should rejoice.

Instead of being forced to hide, we have our own sites, community events and publications. We can walk openly without fear. Discretion is still necessary, but more for sociological reasons than safety. I like to be cautious but never closeted. Knowing one's audience gives them what they need to better communicate and avoid dangers.

Modern magic can exist with technology. They're friends in my eyes. No one should have to choose between connecting with nature and enjoying science and technology. Both co-exist well in my home.

We implemented no-tech days to get away from the pressures of notifications and clear the body and soul of that impulse to check for emails, texts and posts. I work a lot and often need sacred walks with my family. Getting back to the woods without any "devices" reminds me of where I come from. It strengthens my intuition and provides inner peace.

The land of the connected has different merits. I do not go online to find myself, but to find others. Share a little bit of the warmth and human connection that binds all lives together. This is what got my writing career going.

I researched Pagan websites and publications to submit my writing to after first being asked to share my experiences through writing. I'll admit I cheated, I looked up a couple of notable Pagan authors and browsed their writing credits. This is the best place to find more outlets.

Writers often list where their work has been displayed. This leads to various companies that shined onscreen. Llewellyn came up most often. They are a major Pagan publisher with a variety of material on a vast array of subjects. I recommend looking up their titles.

Second was: The Witches' Voice. Also known as Witchvox, this website is a social media platform for all things witchy and Pagan. From essays and book reviews, to event listings, this site is a mecca of Paganism. Writers do not have to be well-known to get published here, just respectful.

Reading the insights from other Pagans helped me grow more confident. We see big brassy witches in movies who make no apologies and feel insignificant in comparison. Outdated portrayals are the death of great cinema.

At Witchvox it's okay to express fears, message writers and find your way without judgement. My first accepted piece of work was published in June of 2011. It had been rejected by a few other Pagan publications and it's not my best work. I fear it rubbed some people the wrong way, but my intentions were merely observational.

I learned from the feedback. I continued exploring my powers through meditation, lifestyle and faith. Since then I've published fifteen other articles. Every one of them has brought more questions to my inbox. I've met with some criticism and a wealth of love and understanding.

Beyond the writing, the book reviews provide details on new releases. It promotes lesser known titles that I would have otherwise missed out on. Authors can submit links to their books and be listed as well. My love of the written word warms to this (especially in a culture of pay-for-promos).

It is free to sign up, but members can sponsor the site for a minimal annual fee. Witchvox does not have ads or try to push agendas like other social media sites. It is all about giving us a voice, a place to find each other so we can be strong together when it's impossible to go it alone.

The best feature of The Witches' Voice is the event finder and Pagan shop listings. Users can look up every known Pagan/New Age shop in any area of the globe. The U.S. is filled with them. These shops often host events and/or advertise Pagan community gatherings.

The events finder helps direct Pagans to Pride Day celebrations and pagan Picnics. I'm lucky to be a Saint Louis native. Our June festival is a huge two-day event. People of all faiths are always welcome. The crowd is full of unique personalities.

I once met a lady named, "Story," while signing books at the St. Louis Pagan Picnic. I've also enjoyed the freedom of fair trade. Money is tight sometimes. I get that. I'd rather trade my books for something special than bank on sales.

I've traded for other books, handmade soaps and lotions, all sorts of items. My most treasured trade was with a young Romani man (commonly knowns as gypsy) who gifted me a crystal in exchange for my first children's book. He sealed it with a kiss on my cheek.

It sits at my desk as I type these words.

The gift of meeting face-to-face and supporting each other is more valuable than any monetary funds. Supporting other Pagans or positive influencers of any faith leads to extraordinary bonds.

What about when you can't make it?

Twitter, Facebook, Instagram, Pinterest, Tumblr and more all have their own Pagan communities. From tweets about ritual, to full moon blessings, the posts keep coming. Some are personal. Getting acquainted with other Pagans online can lift spirits when they dip low.

But I have a few rules that I think are important to always stress.

1. **Keep it Light**: Revealing too much feeds trolls. Getting overly political or preachy turns people off. I learned this, again, through trial and error. We all say things we probably should have kept to ourselves, but the best fun is had when joking around and indulging our individuality.

2. **Be Careful**: No matter how safe the tech wall feels, there are strangers on the other end and unfortunately not all of them are good people. DON'T give out personal information like phone numbers and addresses. It's not safe. Again, speaking from experience here.

3. **Don't Get Carried Away**: Social media panders to egotism. Remember to remain humble and loyal to those who treat you right. You'll have highs and lows online.

4. **Going Online is Like Going Out in Public**: Everything you post is like walking it down the street for anyone to see, except the internet never forgets. I've had internet mobs come after me for saying something offensive. It's harsh. Whether it's misinterpreted or you just had a bad day, it happens. This is where freedom of speech and the importance of disconnecting come in handy.

5. **Remember the Real World**: No matter how good or bad you are treated online, take a walk outside. Get away from screens to remind yourself that people, in general, can get along. The media is always painting gruesome pictures. Yes, the world has problems, but sometimes you have to go to a park or library to witness a diverse group of people coexisting peacefully to combat the divisive nature of internet outrage.

Once you get to know people better, exchanging info is cool. I met my husband on twitter. I never thought I would be that person. He was an artist and I'm a writer. It just happened. I call it: love at first type. But we built a lot of trust before meeting.

Finding the people who best mesh with you takes time. Energy. The connections we make influence the course of our lives. Balance reaching out with protecting yourself. It's surprising how these technologies run their course.

Kitchen Witch

Once you find your groove, you'll find out your specific gifts. This is not a fantasy novel reference. No romance either. This is a truth.

Everyone has their own strengths and weaknesses. Finding and embracing what comes naturally will aid you in all avenues of life. Like I mentioned before, my sister grows things without trying. My mom has the sight. She passed some of that onto us, but it's not nearly as strong. It's more of a slight ability.

We can all practice at different elements and build stronger connections in the corners of the magical philosophies. That's not what I'm talking about. A true spiritual gift is something a person is born with. It lives in them. It refuses to become dormant. It sneaks out no matter how hard one tries to fight it – if they so choose to.

I'm a messy person and ever since I was born I enjoyed playing in mud and trying to serve live worms to my friends when we played house. My mother came from a loving woman who had no idea how to concoct beautiful healthy meals. Because of that I was raised on a lot of prepackaged junk.

I thought that was how it was supposed to be. We don't often question our lifestyles until we're old enough to look beyond them. The fast food industry was booming. Most parents worked and struggled to balance meals with challenging schedules.

Our culture has full on accepted this societal shift. It's depicted in books, movies and some songs. We shifted to a throwaway take-out people. This may suit a majority of busy individuals, but I recognized this when I took a simple home economics class in high school. I needed an extra class and it looked easy.

When I stepped into the kitchen the first day, it was like entering a new world. The counters welcomed me. The shiny pots and pans smiled. My teacher didn't worry about students making a mess as long as we cleaned up as we went and left our work space as clean as we found it.

During that period, I mixed, poured and cooked like a pro. My teacher applauded my efforts. I enjoyed it. Taking the time to beat some dough gave me a place to turn my frustrations into productivity.

Before then, I had baked cookies a few times, but this held a different recipe. It dripped with magic. I took what I learned with me. Those first attempts turned into new recipes, new experiments.

My meditations and spells began to shape and mold new outlets. I found myself condensing steps to save time. Canned ingredients no longer appeased me. My spirit longed to utilize fresh foods and make everything from scratch.

When I got married and became a mother, I knew my way around a kitchen. Instead of just making meals, I poured my energies into everything I made. The electricity built in my fingertips and soaked into each dish like it was meant to.

I didn't realize it until my meals cured bad moods. I suspected when I could aid my husband on a bad day. Not in the usual "eat something because your blood sugar is low" way, but in a "flip of the switch, one bite is all it takes" kind.

During this phase of experimenting, I began to feel compelled to bake banana bread. I didn't wish to eat it. Something inside me said it should be shared. Instead of questioning this purpose, I trusted that inner voice.

I made the bread and sent it to work with my husband so his co-workers could enjoy it. Within a month a family friend died. We went to the funeral and caught up with people.

Then I got another urge to bake this bread. I did so, and a month later there was another funeral to go to. It happened four or five times before I glanced at the recipe and wondered if it was some kind of intuition.

When the need to bake it again returned I hesitated. "Could this mean someone else was going to die soon?" I wondered.

My daughter was three years old and helping me in the kitchen at that point. I adored her help. She'd taken to mixing with me as soon as she could control a spoon. I asked her if she thought I was being silly and she laughed. "You're always silly, but not wrong."

The wisdom of babies.

We set to work. While mixing the batter I asked her, "Who do you think it will be, if someone dies?"

Her experience with funerals and meditation had gifted her with a healthy acceptance of death. "Grandma Rose."

I froze. "Why would you say that?" I gaped at her.

She shrugged. "Just thought it."

My mother in law, Rose, was not sick. She had a few known health problems, but nothing that would indicate she would not be with us much longer. A month later, she died. She had developed a rare condition that was difficult to detect.

I spent a great deal of time consoling my daughter. Although she didn't fear death and understood that grandma couldn't live forever, she blamed herself for knowing beforehand. Many of us do this. Any witch or Pagan who has predicted something difficult can attest to experiencing guilt.

No matter where your gifts lay, do not mistake knowledge for fault. Over time she came to terms with it. We baked more banana bread when the time called and attended the services that followed.

Now when we get the "banana bread sense" we breathe deep and hope that whoever is passing on finds a peaceful end. It is always within two-degrees of our family and friends. Instead of fearing it, or growing upset, we embrace the inevitable and enjoy the time we have.

The bread offers comfort. It usually makes people smile even when they don't want to. Our talents are meant to be shared because they can help others. I cook, not because I have to. I cook because it is an important aspect of my being. Food enhances love. It allows us to stop and enjoy the little things, to be thankful to be alive.

If you wish to explore your culinary skills, I suggest starting small. I prefer to cook from scratch but not everyone has to. Find new foods, healthier foods that nourish your body and enhance the mind. Even the bitterest vegetables can be enjoyable with the right combinations of spices and sauce.

Certain spoons and spatulas will become trusted friends. Frequently used recipes transform into staples you long for. Not everyone has a gift for cooking, but if you find it boosts your energies, funnel them into what you create. Get your hands dirty. Have fun. You are a conductive being. Harness that power and transform it into something you love.

Fate

The spiritual lifestyle trusts fate. Putting down one's guard to emerge in the future with an open heart eases this. It is yet another challenge all humans face. How can someone feel safe and comforted when the unknown lurks in every shadow?

Utilizing natural gifts is an aid, as well as mediation and self-awareness, but fate goes beyond that. Sybil Leek wrote about charting the stars, how everything was written in them for anyone to see, if they educated themselves properly. Society chalks this up as nonsense due to cynicism and the new religion of disbelief.

It's as if a movement to only trust science is fueling everything now. As a biology nerd, I love science. It's intelligent to look to facts and constants in order to gain a solid grasp of reality. It's strange to write that in a spiritual book about magic and energies, but science and magic are friends. They always have been, we just misinterpret their relationship.

Consciousness is just another aspect of life. It's real. It is always being studied, but the spiritual is more complicated. No matter how far technology and measured sciences go, we cannot find the answers to everything. When studying the well-known aspects of human reproduction, scientists are still unable to pin-point the exact moment of conception when an egg is fertilized because sometimes the cells react right away, sometimes after twenty-four hours, and sometimes they do not begin changing until up to seventy-two hours after the sperm meets the egg.

I love that. No matter how much we know, we can never know everything. That gives me hope for everyone. Knowledge may be power, but how one utilizes their knowledge is the generator.

The greatest life lessons come from experience. Books are helpful, and good teachers encourage students to interpret things for themselves. I would never dispute that. What I'm talking about is wandering through life ready to learn while listening. Not with our ears or eyes, but our spirit.

Have you ever just felt something?

An answer screamed within you, burned to be known?

That is a spark ready to ignite the fire within. The universe speaks to us through our senses. We see patterns for a reason. We live them.

We are but a great maze of complex souls that interweave throughout our lives. This is why some people give us chills and some make us sweat. Our chemical makeup controls those bodily reactions, but if you listen to them, set aside embarrassment or reservations, it goes deeper. Every sensation is linked to the core of who we are.

It's vital that we listen to and register these links. Get to know them. Instead of hiding from our fears and mental deficiencies, we need to test them, learn to control them. I used to be the worst hot-head. My bipolar would switch gears so quick I scared my mother.

It was not until I stopped making excuses and realized only I could flip the switch and contain my madness, that I saw myself for who I could be. Meditation helps. Finding talents and gifts to balance negative energy is another key to unlocking your freedom-of-self.

The big one, the doozie that pulls it all together, is fate. Acknowledging and greeting the world and the potential of your path helps. We can run from who we are or find love inside. Many of the world's common problems stem from self-hatred or egotism. It is self-hatred that breeds mistrust; egotism produces disdain for others.

They may seem like opposites, but they come from the same place, a lack of balance. Love is balanced. Love sees others for their mistakes and still cares. Love knows that beauty is not on the surface but much deeper.

Enough with the hippy-dippy lovies. I can get carried away on that subject. When I say love, I do not mean the modern ideal. Not soulmates and romantic gesture garbage, but the inner light that looks for reasoning and understanding.

The voice inside is smarter than we know. It leads us to see past pain, anger, fear and trauma. It needs to be tuned like an instrument to sing louder. This is why nature walks mean so much to me.

Technological devices have a weird relationship with me. I accept their help when necessary but prefer to work as primitively as possible. I find fate leads me better when I step away from man-made conveniences.

Call it the old Gods; call it Mother Nature clearing away an army of stresses our ancestors never faced. Whatever it is, I don't care. What matters is the method in which to use it to better ourselves. Instinct.

We like to believe that we're more advanced than our instincts, that we don't need them anymore, but they're more important than ever. Looking to the sky or the trees helps clear my head. Exercising my body through hiking with only the music of the wind and birds calls upon my inner voice, it sharpens my instincts.

Hunter

I learned this when hunting and fishing with my father as a kid. Getting back to our roots and being forced to practice methods used by many people before us drew something out of me, made it readily available. It prepared me to take care of myself in any situation.

I fell into the trap of villainizing hunters before that. It's easy to look at a man or woman with a gun and assume they enjoy killing. After going through the extensive Missouri Conservation Program and doing some of my own research, I found the necessity. Regulating the deer population prevents disease and starvation among these gentle creatures. Most hunters look toward the creatures they kill as symbols of life and vitality. There is a respect and love held for them.

When I killed my first deer a rush of exhilaration overcame me. I was able to provide food for my family. I was able to gift other deer a longer healthier life.

I nearly fell over myself getting to the body. My dad had to hold me back. He made me take in what I had done. We then walked softly.

Coming upon the dead animal, he left me with it for a few minutes and it was then that I knelt down and cried.

I did not shed tears of regret. They slipped from my eyes because of the nature of the food chain. I ran my hands over the fur and thanked the deer for giving its life. Meat does not have to be included in our diets but there are many benefits, especially for men. Women are better equipped for abstaining from meat based on our bodies' ability to store more fat.

Even so, I find meat to be sacred at feasts. Years later, while still respecting others hunting rights, I became a vegetarian. As a high-energy sporty woman, my muscles felt weaker and so I allowed myself only fish. That pescatarian diet served me well. I'd never felt healthier.

Now in my mid-thirties, I cook a lot of vegetarian meals but do eat some fish and other meats a few times a week. My body has never responded better. My energies are at their best. I also thank the animals who gave their lives so I can live better.

It is a sort of Pagan prayer. A way to remember the life and its place in this world. Everything has its place here, even humans. I find it disheartening that self-hatred is represented so widely. Many people blame humanity for all the world's troubles.

Yes, we have a massive effect on this Earth and we need to work together to do better, but just writing us off as some kind of plague is shallow and discredits all our great work. In order to find balance, we need to see the bigger picture. Deep within, I know that Mother Nature can knock us back if needs be. It's presumptuous of us to believe that we, one species, can destroy an entire planet completely. Sure we can cause much damage, but the Gods do reprimand us.

I feel that in my bones, and have witnessed it in life. Listening to the energies surrounding us leads to better outcomes.

Gatherer

If hunting is not an option, or even wandering forests is difficult, people can employ other ancient means of connecting with fate. The hunter-gatherer imprints are still apparent in us. Gathering is not just about plucking berries, it's about finding the materials and foods that build a solid lifestyle.

I'm very territorial. Everything that comes into my house to stay has to hold the right meaning. It must serve a purpose and have a respected place.

Instead of just accepting presents (like a nice person would do), I must feel them out. I don't hold with mass consumerism or products that are bad for the environment. What I "gather" in my life also gives my inner voice more volume.

I minimize plastics. Anything made from the "blood of the earth" reeks of death to me. I hate the feel of it and other artificial items. Solid woods are favored, but even cardboard, paper, glass and metals are welcome, depending on how they are manufactured.

All of these come from the earth. Some are mined. What we take needs to be minimized so we give enough to allow our planet to flourish. No, I don't live in a mini home. As cool as that sounds, I doubt I'd find balance drowning in three kids and tripping over my dog and other animal friends.

I also refuse to ever own a giant home, though. My grandparents raised my mom and seven siblings in a home that had maybe 1000 square feet. They had a giant family by today's standards, and a small house. Nowadays people look for twice to four times that amount of space with a quarter of the people. That blows my mind.

What are they doing with all that space? Do they even see each other every day?

There is a younger generation afraid to buy a house because they see these unrealistic standards and it doesn't equate. Getting back to simplicity and finding or building smaller homes will help us allow stronger communities for all levels of incomes.

The word community holds a lot of power in itself. When people "gather" together in a smaller setting we can do big things. Neighborly "gathering" used to be common, the more I engage in my community and talk to people in my sister's as well, the more I see that we lost that along the way.

When I was a kid we were poor. Not "I can't eat out every night" poor, but "we lived off of Ramen and my mom had to write bad checks to keep a roof over our heads" poor. But we knew all our neighbors. We had to. It was the only way to find success.

The rise in bigger houses with their own backyard pools and playgrounds gave people the freedom to abstain from social gatherings. Isolating ourselves sounds nice sometimes, but it does little for connection and fulfillment. My children are allowed a tire swing, but if they want to slide and climb monkey bars and sit on a traditional swing, we walk to the park so we can gather with others and enjoy socializing.

This approach is also applied to swimming, which we do at a local park by the river, because I prefer natural bodies of water, and sports. If not metaphorically gathering ourselves with others, there is also a strange sense-of-purpose in cleaning up the yard or collecting trash along sidewalks and roads.

Bending down to pick up trash and clean up the grass is another act that fine tunes a direct connection with the energies around us. It is as satisfying as harvesting crops from a backyard garden or picking wildflowers before they die.

Lover

Indulging our wild sides eases pent up aggression. It allows us to tame ourselves when necessary. It also opens the mind toward higher ideas. When one is at one with themselves, nature, and their lifestyle, they will find symbols in the strangest places. Events come together; strangers can serve as guides in your walk-of-life.

Trust becomes possible.

Love expands and the ability to empathize and respect every side of any argument will blossom. Perfection wasn't made for this world. Trials still present themselves. But throughout the harshest events, I've found the right people, places and timing.

Not everyone and everything is meant to stay in your life for long. Some people are mere poets with the sole purpose of lending you the phrase you need to see the patterns that guide you further on your path. Others create bonds so deep they entangle loyalty and life-long love.

It's not easy to differentiate. We don't have to. The answers come in time. Patience must be found. The Gods like a good laugh. Sometimes they laugh at us and we must learn to find good humor in everything to survive without withering. It spreads love and keeps us alive.

Healing Powers

The "evil witch" troupe is so played out. I get it. It's entertaining. It's a great way to scare people into behaving or conforming for whatever reason.

It is strange to me that despite the giving nature of most magical practices, Pagans and witches have been villainized throughout much of history. One of the main aspects of honing one's path is learning how to creative positive change. Whether for one's self or others, spiritual knowledge (like all knowledge) desires balance.

The healing powers of magic are less, "eye of newt," and more centralized. Herbs and medicinal ingredients do sometimes play a role in combating illness and disease, but I find energy levels and visualization to be just as important for effective results.

Health plays a huge role in that stability. If you don't take care of yourself you cannot look after anyone else. Motherhood taught me that.

Energy Transference

Keeping in good health takes practice. It is work. Everything a person eats matters. Foods packed with vitamins and minerals from the earth fuel bodies with top grade nutrients. They boost the immune system, and subsequently boost personal power and magical energies.

There is a reason traditional mothers forced their children to eat their vegetables.

Veggies, fruits, berries and nuts leave a body working in top condition. Lean meats offer strength and vitality. A proper diet cleans the system.

Exercise teaches a person how to listen to their body. We learn to differentiate between "good" pains and "bad" pains. "Good" pains are the ones like stiffness, soreness and tenderness that wear off in a short timeframe. "Bad" pains stab, shock, jolt and don't stop.

Knowing the difference will aid anyone just as understanding the difference between pain and discomfort. Discomfort is annoying; it might hold slight pains but is manageable. It's a sensation that one can survive through. It's often described as pressure. Pain is more defined. It hurts enough to make people stop and take notice.

In a society of painkillers, people seem to forget that pain has a purpose. It is there to tell us when we're ailing so we can pinpoint the issue and potentially alleviate it. Taking over the counter pills to dull the sensation can lead to long-lasting injuries that never heal. It also masks our ability to assess our situation and determine when to see a doctor.

I admit I have a strong phobia of pharmaceuticals and big pharma. What works for me is not the answer for everyone, but limiting medications limits side-effects. Just like in magic, there is always a price to pay. I prefer the karmic returns of magical energies because they are honest and balanced.

When diet and exercise do not prevent illness, I prefer to turn to my healing powers. These can be learned. They come to some naturally, others must practice often. With everything, power and energy levels are the key.

But how does one heal themselves when they are ailing?

Mind-over-matter drives the outcome. My mother put all her faith in this principal when I was young. We often didn't have health insurance and so she would tell my sister and I not to get hurt or we'd have to heal ourselves.

When I was nine years old I got sick a lot. It was during this period that I began focusing my mind to centralize where my life source sprang from and encourage it to overcome whatever sickness left me lying in bed. This became common.

Through the years, I expanded on the philosophy. Once I studied enough Eastern philosophies and found my way to Pagan texts, the answers grew clearer. When striving to heal myself I follow a simple set of steps that can easily be reproduced before turning to spell-work (spell-work is not the answer to everything and I always approach it with caution).

Step 1: Lie down (simple enough).

Step 2: Control your breathing and clear your mind as if preparing to meditate.

Step 3: Feel yourself out and decide where your spiritual spark is strongest, where your energies come from. It is just beneath my sternum for me, but may be closer to the belly button, heart, or located at the head for others (it's different for everyone).

Step 4: Fixate on those energies. Block everything else out. Then visualize your energies flowing from the center with a glowing light. This light may take on a specific color or not. Mine is neon blue (you can close your eyes or keep them opened; I always close mine).

Step 5: Make those energies extend to your arms and down through your fingers. See the light slipping over the skin. Place your hands over the area in need. Feel the warmth of the light take over. Push it out through your fingers and will it to fix the issue, not the symptoms.

Step 6: Relax and ground yourself. Make sure to nourish your body and mind afterwards. Healthy foods, books, art films and nature walks will revive your energies.

Step 7: Repeat once a day as needed.

This cannot work without faith. If the practitioner doesn't believe in themselves, this approach, magic, or energy transference, it will not be successful. It takes all types of strength.

Tending Others

If and when comfortable with self-healing, it may be necessary to help others. The main rule to follow when using magic on someone else (helpful or no) is to always get consent first. If someone doesn't trust it or wish to go that route then it's not meant to be.

I broke this rule once in my life and though it saved a child from dying, it also took a loved one from us unexpectantly to maintain balance. That was not my goal. I thought I held more control than I did. Unable to perform a solid energy transference, I turned to spellwork. During this ritual, the energies wove themselves in a different direction.

I was not specific enough. I had not spoken with the parents first. I am glad to see the child thriving now but cannot look at them without remembering the loss. It is a lesson that remains with me always.

Healing spells are complex and personal. I prefer energy transference instead. It takes more time than self-care. One must meditate and prepare their mind, body and spirit to extend these courtesies. The steps are the same as listed in the previous section, but require focus and an ability to let go of internal blockers.

It is a type of reverse grounding. Building up the energy to heal another person means shutting off one's selfish nature. Quieting the mind to tend to another's needs takes practice. I'm a mother, so my maternal bonds make it easier when my children are in need. Helping my husband also keeps me in good practice, but what truly helped me harness this ability is my work with animals.

As a child I nursed sick strays. In my teens I took in unwanted animals. My twenties led me to animal care work. I found it easier for me to put aside my thoughts and concerns when taking care of animals. From dogs and cats to opossums or monkeys, their instincts guided mine.

The natural world is much slower than ours. It is quieter too. I had to train myself to exude a calm gentle nature. Working to build trust with a creature who does not understand why it's in pain will prepare a person for anything.

Establishing trust with a patient, human or animal, breeds energy. Have the person sit or lie down in whatever position is most comfortable for them and perform steps 2–7 as before. With animals, you will need to be more involved.

Animals cannot say, "Yes, please heal me." But they can cry for help. They whimper or moan. They communicate with their movements, their eyes. If a person studies these behaviors enough, they will know when to intervene and when to step back.

Simply holding the creature close will do, in the case of the former. Then steps 2–7 will come naturally.

We all hold different energies. No matter how they are used, a person must ground themselves afterward. The body cannot handle such highs and lows. It is like mixing uppers and downers. The heart needs transition. The mind must decompress.

After healing another, sharing a healthy snack while raising the feet up is a good technique. So is singing or petting an animal. Meditation is also a great method, but often puts me to sleep if I get too comfortable after such taxing work.

That can lead to unguided journeys through the subconscious. For most people, it's not a good idea. Even when extending our energies far beyond ourselves, we still need a way back.

Cosmic Healing

Energy transference is not just for healing individuals. It can be strengthened and focused to heal communities, ecosystems and large groups, but there is little ability to gain approval from all involved. I love nature and all its beings. I see destruction in some areas and wish to change it.

The best purposes to direct at larger entities are transferences that offer love and understanding. Anything beyond that will either backfire, or create only temporary solutions. Remember, magic cannot solve everything. It is not some fix-all-elixir that brings about happy endings. It is a method, one that should be approached with scientific caution.

Anything that draws from your energies is serious, especially the unexplainable.

The Supernatural

Skeptics are everywhere. Leave them to their truths. If they wish to ignore the unexplainable, let them. The rest of us will have more fun.

Not every cold spot is a cause for alarm. Sometimes a light flickers because of electrical issues or dying bulbs. Many scientific reasons explain what people mistake for supernatural experiences. I won't deny that. What I can attest to is the presence of spirits and areas that harbor explosive energies.

I have seen them. I have lived them. It's not nearly as exciting as it's portrayed in fiction, but does lead to many questions and sensations. They leave an impression.

Ghosts

In movies, people wander a dark hall. Their back is exposed. They hear some creepy noise, turn and scream in the face of danger.

Really?

Who writes this stuff?

It makes for great comedy. I love laughing at ridiculous horror films, but my experiences with apparitions have all been relatively tame. There are two main schools of thought as to why real ghosts or spirits, whatever one wishes to call them, are not the violent monsters some people still fear.

1. Time is not consistent and the fabric can be misshapen. This theory suggests that ghosts do not consciously exist in the present, but are just a memory replaying before our eyes. It explains why many known

apparitions repeat the same actions, remain in the same place and don't often interact with those living in the present.

2. Spirits do not always know they are dead or do not wish to move on to what comes after death. This belief requires some faith in an afterlife. It may seem like wishful thinking to cynical atheists, but it explains why some apparitions walk freely where they wish, find certain people to communicate with, and return during the thinning of the veil between worlds on October thirty-first.

Both can and do exist, based on what I've experienced. The first is less individual-based and generally proves to be an issue with the location itself. Certain spaces don't adhere to the rules of physics as we know them. These are sometimes known as vortexes and have nothing to do with ghosts, but rather a location that twists time or holds a portal that warps certain elements of reality.

That "don't go in there!" room, is more likely a vortex than a haunting.

By contrast, the second take is all about the spirit. Those are the "real" ghosts. The lost souls or visiting relatives who come to check in on loved ones.

I have never understood why someone would fear ghosts. They cannot hurt anyone who is unafraid, and the only way they can is by using fear as a weapon. The simplest comparison I've found is feral dogs. Like wild strays, ghosts can be untrusting, angry, frustrated, territorial and stubborn.

I refuse to say that being nice will fix this. Sometimes kindness can't help a person. Often, it takes a firm hand.

Ghosts are also like children. They can throw tantrums, mess with your stuff, or annoy a person until they go crazy.

The only way to handle them is with calm resolve. There is some kind of entity living in my current house. Even my in-laws who are non-believers got freaked out when my husband's guitar strummed itself during our move.

I didn't believe it at first, as I didn't witness it and I hate jumping to uneducated conclusions. But after settling in, I've heard loud drum beats playing beneath our bedroom, had plenty of things knocked off of shelves and counters, cabinet doors opened on their own, the kitchen trashcan knocked over, glasses that shattered for no reason, and the list goes on.

I don't take kindly to rudeness. I cleansed our house when we moved in, but that helps secure the area and combat vortexes. It does not prevent a resident ghost from remaining. It can nudge them to leave, but our unexpected roommate is not ready and I am in no rush to expel it.

I've made it clear that we can share the space and, for the most part, things have toned down. Unfortunately, my husband is not used to this activity. He also suffers from a bad memory so when things quiet down for a while and then we have another incident, his reaction eggs the spirit on and they play off of each other.

This behavior leads me to think it's either a child or a dog. We know the previous owners buried a dog in the backyard. We sometimes hear barking in the basement when our dog is asleep. He does not like going downstairs alone and avoids the closest corner to the gravesite.

When researching the house's history, no human deaths have been found. It figures. Only I could end up being haunted by a dog. I quite enjoy it, and it is hilarious to me.

I named it Bill and when it knocks over the garbage, I laugh and shout, "Please get out of my kitchen, Bill," just like I do when our living dog sneaks into the kitchen while I'm cooking. It's our norm.

Bill responds and behaves accordingly. He still messes with my husband at times, but it makes the children laugh.

The key rules to remember are:

Rule #1: Be polite. This Golden Rule applies to everyone, not just the living. Rudeness begets rudeness and won't stop with a ghost.

Rule #2: Set aside all fears. There is no place for shrieking, screaming or running away when dealing with ghosts. Displays of fear give them power. It feeds their energies.

Rule #3: Stand firm. Be firm and forceful. Not bossy or overly emotional, but strong and commanding as if training a dog or keeping a child in line.

Rule #4: Exercise patience. Like all beings, even ghosts have feelings. They often feel trapped and alone. When they act out it is to get attention. Do not feed into that cycle.

Listing rules for interacting with ghosts is not something I ever foresaw.

My previous experiences were more mystical. They held ambience and intrigue. When I was pregnant with my first child, my grandfather (who had been dead for years) checked in on me. I sensed him for days beforehand. For most of that October my skin pricked. My eye was constantly drawn to the hallway between my living room and the bedrooms.

A powder blue light shined from it in the corner of my eye. Changing angles didn't disturb the glow. A lot of people told me they had seen things while they were pregnant, so I wrote it off at first. Vision is known to change due to the hormones as well. Something about the fluttering kicks inside me had made me extra observant and paranoid at times, but after a few weeks, I couldn't ignore the hue that taunted my peripheral vision.

Every time I turned to stare at it, it dimmed and faded. As we neared Samhain, it held longer each time. At the end of October, I saw the faint outline of my grandfather, barely visible. Strange things have happened in my family before. I often "saw things" as a kid, but this wasn't a midnight vision that could be written off as a dream. It was mid-afternoon. I felt him all around me. I could smell him. It was perfectly natural, as if he just stopped in for a visit.

I said, "Hi grandpa,." and smiled. I stood to move toward him. The lights flickered and he was gone. I got the feeling he didn't expect me to acknowledge him.

Before then, I had only felt presences or seen them in dreams. The dream world contains a bridge that can be walked over easier. In dreams we accept truth much quicker than in the waking world.

Ghosts seem like dreams at times. There are stories of them everywhere, yet some people do not even believe they exist. Thankfully I was raised to believe in the possibility of everything. Doubt is allowed to wander freely, but because I look for the unseen, it finds me more often than not.

How I process and learn from each experience is what matters. This is how I have come to question the validity of hauntings. Humans often mislabel what they do not understand. Not every apparition is a ghost or a spirit. It is helpful to know the difference.

Vortexes

Unlike ghosts, vortexes are places where time and space move differently or the energies give off specific vibes. Some houses feel alive. Some lands watch us as if they are living beings. Again, there are two takes on this.

1. When a building is created, it absorbs some of the workers' energies. It obtains an aura in this way. I first encountered this while visiting construction sites with my father. The ever-changing feel of each plot grew as it became developed. It was as if the houses were being birthed instead of built.

2. Some areas are situated in a perfect spot with just the perfect position, surroundings, minerals or metals and rocks, that they hold their own realities. Myths about stepping into fae realms exist for a reason.

The first is not a vortex but a collective outcome of continuous work. Every house holds some kind of "heart" to me. They develop their own character, but they are not actually alive nor do they contain a spirit.

The second definition gives some insight to vortexes. The science behind this theory is shaky at best. Some give off energies that crash computers, disrupt signals or overload power systems. Others cause mental issues in people, with long-term or even short-term associations. Whether an accumulation of drastic events left behind some invisible mark, or the spot itself was born charged, is often unclear, but anyone who has visited or dared to live in such a place can attest to the reality of the disposition.

My limited experience with a few potential vortexes does not make me any kind of expert. I cannot claim to be a guide. Still, my encounters have shaped how I approach "haunted" buildings.

The first instance was during the previously mentioned trespassing expedition when, as a teen, I went to an abandoned nursing home with my original coven. This left me catatonic until a spell brought me back. I remember being locked in my own head. It wasn't fun.

Instead of screaming inside an unresponsive body, as horror depictions would insist, the sensation was less dramatic. My will to control myself dissipated. It was as if the ability to care evaporated and left my mind floating inside a useless body.

Once I was revived, then the terror hit me. Waking to the reality of what happened flooded me with questions. Those unanswered worries are what left the biggest impression.

Reexamining the memories, I recall being warned that the basement was noted to house dark secrets. Rumors of abuse and unwarranted punishments leaked from circle to circle. It is possible that those unfortunate residents' pain and suffering remained like a stain in that area and it seeped into me as I neared it.

All people have the ability to feel for others through empathy. There is a growing movement of self-proclaimed "empaths." I would never label myself as such, but have been known to share other's sensations.

This would explain the feeling of helplessness and the disconnect from my own body. The human brain is a complex work of mastery. The symbols drawn on the walls and floor were indecipherable to everyone present that day, but they could have also had an effect.

I will probably never know.

What I learned from that night is the art of protection. Protection charms work. They cannot be forgotten. They are a beacon that clears away uncertainty.

Protections

Full protection is proactive. One must take action to prevent harm by either charging a charm, performing a spell or sealing a circle. Circles exist for a reason. They represent maternal love, the womb; in essence, the protections of that energy.

When casting a circle, you are calling on the nurturing forces of existence to blanket you from the dangers of the world. Salt is the neutralizing agent. It is the physical connection to our bodies. Water as well. A pure circle is sprinkled with salt to lay the foundation, and water to consecrate it.

Blessed water is best. Unlike Christian holy waters, anyone can meditate on their chalice and transfer cleansing power into it. The circle must be cast around you. Doorways are sometimes acceptable but not recommended.

Once cast, the air will feel different. Flesh and mind are no longer vulnerable to angry spirits or dark forces.

But one cannot live in a circle forever. Spells can aid with this. There are countless books on protection spells but the only one that ever mattered to me requires nothing more than a vivid mind. Like the healing practices mentioned in the previous chapter, it centers around visualization.

As a child I saw things I could not explain. I had to learn to keep myself safe. I would close my eyes and find that spiritual center under my rib-cage. A glowing light sparked from there. I made it expand like a balloon, growing the sphere around my body until completely surrounded, enclosed in a bubble of my own doing.

This tactic would have served me in the abandoned nursing home, but I do not adhere to hiding in circles or balls of light anymore. The concept tires me. Instead, my preferred method is charms.

Like most witches, I do not wear much jewelry. I prefer my body to be as free as possible. My wedding ring is all I refuse to take off.

Necklaces, bracelets, anklets, toe rings, belly rings, nose rings, earrings, eyebrow rings all look cool. They have their own purposes to individual people, but they have little place in magic, unless charged for a purpose. My rule is one charm at a time.

I sometimes don a simple pentacle (also known as a pentagram). When necessary, I charge it during full moon rituals to protect me. Most protections do not last forever. There is no such thing as an unbreakable spell. Some are stronger than others, and some require counter acts to create balance, but protections usually need to be recharged or at least maintained.

My rite is simple. I set my alter for the Moon. Light the candles and have one carved out with protection symbols to get me in the correct mindset. After casting a circle and welcoming the Gods and the elements, I dangle my pentacle in the candle's fire while chanting for protections. The words sometimes come out like a song, but they do change.

Once burning hot, I lay the metal charm before the candles and finish my ceremony, leaving the candles to burn out even after I open the circle. This method has guarded me for years now.

Just before every big change in my life the chain breaks and I have to get a new one for my pentacle. I never lose the charm, thankfully. It tells me where it is, even when the chain breaks while I'm away from home.

The last time my chain broke, I got pregnant with my third child. Before that, it was when my husband fell in love with me. Sometimes one must accept the dangers of change in order to move forward. Remaining stagnant is far more perilous and the charms know that. They offer the relief of foresight to ease the coming tide.

Foresight

A bit of "the sight" runs in my family, but it does not have to be hereditary to be harnessed. Most everything unseen is enhanced with meditation and focus. Setting aside time to explore the depths of the mind brings about new revelations.

Looking to the future is something that must be handled with respect and care. How we perceive it effects how it unfolds. Some things cannot be changed or come about when changes backfire. Foresight is not a map to be tampered with. Drawing new lines is not a healthy path.

The entire point of looking into what is to come, is preparation. That's all.

For those of us who are sensitive to their "third eye", as it is sometimes called, gaining control can be a challenge. Most of my visions present themselves in dreams or daydreams. This causes confusion because I have had to train myself to decipher when a dream is not a foreseeable reality. Not every dream is a warning or an insight to the future.

To distinguish between the real and unreal, I don't rely on spell-work or charms. Sometimes I ponder logic and utilize simple mathematical probability. On the rare occasions this fails me, I consult the cards.

Tarot

Tarot cards, like all materials, are just the vessel. They deliver the messages you already contain inside. They draw truth from within.

A person should never just buy a tarot deck and play with it for fun. It will not harm the user, but it hinders the accuracy of the cards. Choosing a deck is important. Receiving one as a gift is best, but if that is not an option, be patient. Wait for the one that calls to you, that you feel you cannot live without.

This better bonds with the practitioner. That bond leads to a connection no impulse buy can achieve. Once a deck is with its master, then comes the act of binding them.

To fully gain the ability to read, one must charge the cards with their energies. This is a simple rite where a person focuses on connecting with that light I have continued to reference, the light from their life source, and shares it with the cards.

Like meditation, this simple act does not ask for much, but can be taxing. It draws forth the subconscious. This allows the user to better interpret each reading.

Instead of looking up manuals or the descriptions within the card box, I was taught to interpret each card based on the feelings it expels.

Study your cards, Get to know them beforehand so you know what each represents to you. No one can duplicate your reading with your cards. That is specific to the owner.

The myth that all cards are the same is hogwash. They are as unique as humanity.

My readings never fail me. Select family and friends have come to swear by them. I have two decks. The first found me when I began my spiritual journey and have been a staple over the years. The second was a gift from my husband. Neither invert.

Many people believe that, if a card is laid upside down, it means the opposite of the usual message. This has never been the case for me. My cards always say what they mean and mean what they say, no backsies.

One spiritualist told me that makes my deck incomplete. She did not know me well and thus offered her expertise, as she was older. I respected her input, but I believe my cards are complete for me. They read the way they do because of my nature.

I do not like liars. I speak my mind (even when I probably shouldn't). I'm very exacting. My cards respond to this and act accordingly. They also get sassy with me when I ask questions they do not appreciate.

My preferred readings are:

1. **The Infamous 3 Card Reading:** Set them before you, left to right. The left is the issue, the middle the resolution, the right is the outcome. Some people do this as past, present and future, but that is too simple for me.

2. **The Diamond:** Set a card down to serve as a center for the others, this is the issue that needs guidance. Place a card directly above it to represent how it affects the person's body. Place the next card to the right of the center to represent how it affects the person's mind. Place another card below the center one to see how it affects the person's spirit. And last, place a card to the left of the center to represent how the issue affects the person's feelings.

I always do these readings together. The first then the second. Always in that order. It lays everything out then eases apprehensions with aid on how to handle the body, mind, spirit and feelings.

Runes

The cards aren't for everyone. My sister preferred runes for many years. There is no deck to shuffle. No cards that may fold or tear.

Runes are more natural. They date back farther and thus offer more basic readings, but more spiritual ones as well. Again, choosing a set is not to be taken lightly. Find something that calls to you, or wait for a gift.

These are easier to charge once obtained, because they are more linked to the physical world. One can sit and hold them in their hands, or hug them to their chest to charge them with personal energies. Chanting fits these more, finding a series of words to connect yourself to the runes and repeating them again and again until the words seem to materialize and draw a link between master and object.

Readings are more interpretive, but that is the point. One who is linked to their runes will see answers in them. My limited knowledge of this practice ends here.

Runes and Tarot are both methods that those born without "the sight" can use freely. It draws more from them and strengthens it. They are best used on a full moon and the Sabbats.

Spells to "see" beyond the known world also exist. They require a lot of preparation and self-awareness, as does scrying. I am less apt to use spell-work to look into the future because I have my dreams and my cards, but I will include the spells I know of in that coming chapter, just as I will detail scrying techniques in the next. The main point of this section is to demystify foresight as some wizardly birthright.

Anyone can attune with nature and see beyond. It comes to some more naturally, but like everything, practice is what truly matters; practice and respect. These qualities guide Pagans and witches. They aid us through hauntings and vortexes. When mingled with our ways, they can lead a spiritualist to extend their services to help others.

A trained spiritualist has the power to protect others from unruly entities. That power comes with a responsibility to help whenever possible.

Cleansings

I studied protection spells and perfected my own rite to charge an object with protective energies. After that I tested myself. I have yet to get lost in my own body again, and even went further, learning to cleanse areas of unwanted existing energies.

This started, like everything else, small. The simple act of creating a circle and cleansing the space within. Salt and water are vital elements. I also bring an instrument with. Some would call it my wand, though I fear that word has been outdated. It is a handcrafted musical instrument sometimes called a Shaman Nut Shaker.

I came across it at random and fell in love with the piece. It called to me. Like many of the books that guided me, it chose me. I did not purchase it intending to include it in my workings. Music holds great sway on my life. My mother said I could sing before I was able to talk. I learned to play guitar at age eight and cannot live without a piano.

Always the songwriter, I imagined the nut shaker would be of some use in my songs. Instead, it held other purposes. It begged to be included in rituals and has over the years directed my energies in new ways.

Sometimes the human body is not the best purveyor of unexplained forces. My instrument, which I jokingly named a woo woo stick, has since clung to that title and wowed me. It came in handy when I studied the art of cleansing one's space to prepare rooms when moving into a new apartment.

I found casting a circle felt more final when directed with the steady vibrations of my instrument. It encouraged more focus, heightened awareness. When my best friend and then boyfriend spoke of fearing certain areas of the movie theatre they worked at, it proved a perfect opportunity to test my knowledge and allow the branches of experience to reach further.

The first thing I did was to charge my pentacle for protection. Then I meditated on a jar of water, dipping my fingertips in to bless it for the upcoming feat. The next day I gathered my woo woo stick with the water and a container of salt, along with some candles and a homemade oil I worked a spell on.

After hours I was led to the back where the hallways snaked around the dying mall it was attached to, called Northwest Plaza. The halls may as well have moaned. They were heavy with despair. Visions of violence and rape taunted my brain.

I laughed. "Well, something sinister happened here."

The freight elevator creeped the employees out to the point that only the managers would ride it. I went there first. Its heavy door loomed threateningly. Its rusty corners glared.

I shrugged and kissed my pentacle. "There is nothing to fear here." I told myself.

This became a chant. A series of words to drive off the negative energies.

"There is nothing to fear here." I lit one of the candles inside the elevator and sprinkled salt and water around the enclosure. I raised my woo woo stick and smiled. "There is nothing to fear here." An overwhelming warmth grew from my sternum through my limbs until it shot out of me and filled the air.

Empowered, I let the rite take over. I stepped out of the elevator and continued to move through the hall sprinkling salt and water, stopping to drip oil, light candles and shake my instrument until the warmth filled the halls.

"There is nothing to fear here." The words became a song. Each syllable drove my energies further. The hall lightened. Its musty crevices no longer leered.

I went the entire length sprinkling salt and water on one side then the other as I walked back, stopping to light candles, drip oil and shake my woo woo stick. The memory draws a laugh. It seems absurd looking back. Me singing to the spaces of that now demolished building.

But whatever I did set a tone. The theater finished in peace. It was shut down within months. The mall itself was torn down.

I pondered my hand in its demise. Could my cleansing have sparked all that happened?

I'm prone to trust fate. Whether I gave it a nudge or not is irrelevant, but the sensations I experienced stayed with me.

My body rang like a charged conductor after performing that ritual. I had to go home, ground myself, and take the night off from life. It gifted me the knowhow to help clear other spaces. When I bought my first house, I did a cleansing of the entire area. Each room, the garage and the entire yard were cleansed and marked with my love.

Cleansings can be performed by anyone, but again I have a set of rules I would suggest others abide by:

1. Protect yourself with a spell or charm beforehand.

2. Work only with areas you have time to put into (it may take a while).

3. Utilize the elements in ways that connect with you (I prefer candles and my instrument).

4. Always carry a neutralizer like salt and/or sage.

5. Trust yourself and the words that come to you (make up your own chants).

6. Never succumb to fear. Negative energies feed off of it and will use it against you.

7. Ground yourself afterwards.

There is no one way to do anything in magic. Personal energies cannot be copied and pasted. They do not fit together like some manufactured product. Caution, intelligence and spunk will lead you where you need to go.

I mention spunk because it should stamp out fear. Unfortunately, everyone succumbs to apprehensions at times which can lead to the potential spiritual phenomenon of possession. This is why protections are so important. I personally do not believe in demons, or the devil from Christian texts, but I have encountered enough negative energies or disturbed spirits that I am not stupid enough to pretend that everything in existence is visible to the eye.

Possession

I believe in the possibility of everything. Life has led me through many unexplained incidents. Though I have yet to encounter possession, I believe this rare phenomenon is possible.

Mental illness, psychosis and even tantrums can probably explain many of the supposed possessions, but having once been trapped in my own body, I am not skeptical of the potential for another to take control of a person. It is a strange concept. One that has horrified cultures for generations.

Instead of impossibly working to prove or disprove the reality of human possession, instead I wish to prevent it. And like cleansing buildings, I believe similar practices are in order to save a person in this predicament.

Prevention

The weak are easy prey. It is nature's way. Harsh and sometimes tragic, that is reality. A weak-willed, weak-minded individual is more susceptible to becoming a vessel for dark forces.

When I was stunned into silence and apathy after visiting an area said to be spiritually dangerous as a teenager, it was during a period in my life where I was still figuring things out. I was exploring faiths and the world around me. Despite my strong-willed personality, my home life was tumultuous and I lacked much familial support.

I was revived within the night, but I needed more protection.

Faith is a great defense. It lends aid in times of unexplained sorrow. It gives light to the dark, and it leads many to enlightenment (true faith, that is, not blind religious hatred of anyone with different aspirations and views).

Faith does not have to be connected to a specific religion. It can extend only to one's self. This is why self-awareness and meditation are so vital to spiritual health. A person without faith is like an empty pea-pod. There are no nutrients, no sustenance.

Education is another defense. Vast knowledge – as in applied intelligence – drives away unwarranted fears. Fearlessness is helpful so long as caution remains. One cannot run blindly through the world without protecting themselves. There are dangers that continue to thrive. But when a person walks without fear, their confidence deters all who prey on the weak.

Health is always a good line of defense. Keeping in shape, eating healthy foods, fasting to cleanse the body and replenishing energies with water instead of sugary drinks, allows the mind to stay focused. It lends control. For any disabled readers, this is not to say that a body with different abilities cannot be or is not healthy. Quite the opposite. No matter what physical obstacles lay before a person, they can find their best nourishment and live well on their own terms.

Charms and spells remain my most trusted protections, but they work better when in conjunction with the other lifestyle methods. Charms are easily created. They serve as a reminder to walk with grace and dignity, but also caution.

I mention caution because it is necessary. Whether I wish for a perfect world where no one ever gets harmed or not, is irrelevant. This is life. Mother Nature set certain rules to warn us and to keep us in line.

Exorcism

Returning a person to themselves is something I only know in concept. If a loved one or friend needed my aid with a possession, I would eagerly rush to their side. I would bring my neutralizers, salt and sage, as well as blessed water, my woo-woo stick, candles and maybe make an oil or balm.

Dark entities thrive on fear and repression. Chants to drive them away will work if the person performing the exorcism is persistent. Never give up and never give in. That is the message of life; it is embedded in the nature of survival. Using this to one's advantage will banish whatever negative energy we must face.

Like cleansing a building, salt and water must be flung onto the "walls" of the person in question: their body. Burning sage will clear the air and any repugnant smells. Dripping protection oils onto a burning candle's flame and chanting while shaking my instrument will create the rhythm, that healing power of a drum circle to create the positive change needed to drive away imbalance or "demons."

Again, this is only a theory, one I am apprehensive to write about too enthusiastically. Curiosity brings out the feline in me. If someday I am able to put these theories into practice I will, of course, write them down and share my findings.

Scrying

Once the spiritual becomes a regular part of a person's lifestyle, once disbelief and skepticism melt away, the physical world becomes a home base. It is where one returns to. It is where we must live, but our minds, bodies and unexplored realms surround us as well.

The concept of time changes with every generation. We know it is relative. It does not always flow at the same rate. It is susceptible to perception and sensitive to the unknown.

This becomes clearer during meditation and other spiritual practices. Time can halt or slow during ritual. It can also be explored through the means of scrying. No I'm not saying everyone should go run out and buy an overpriced crystal ball. That is fantasy.

One cannot just sit down, mumble a few rhymes and magically foresee the future. But with hard work, practice and a trained spirit, images can be pulled from any medium connected to the practitioner.

Crystal balls are made from earth elements. Earth born Pagans and witches may feel drawn to certain rocky materials, gems, geodes and crystals included. Like any ritual materials, finding what suits specific needs is key.

Anyone born under a water sign may see images on the surface of a lake, stream, or river. When practiced enough, a basin of water or mirror is all they should need.

Lovers of air may find signals, messages or entire scenes in dust blown off the ground by windstorms. Tossing leaves or other light objects into the air may present scrying opportunities, but the most consistent air-related option is smoke rising from a fire.

I, myself, am a fire sprite. Born in the heat of the summer, fire guides me. It offers strength. It protects me.

And on rare occasions, it speaks to me.

Building fires give me unbridled joy. Gathering sticks and setting them to kindle over a flame is empowering. I value self-sufficiency above most qualities. There is a calming peace-of-mind that comes with knowing I can take care of myself, no matter what happens.

If I were lost in the woods, I would not perish. If society fell, I could thrive. If the earth shifted and redrew our maps, I could live and still be happy.

Knowing this, I spark new fires and sit before them. I talk to the flames. Laugh as they lick at the wood like a toddler tasting something new. The warmth engulfs not just my skin or nerve endings, but my very being. Everything that I am is alight with life when sitting before a fire. This sometimes leads to visions.

Not always. It doesn't matter how many years one has been practicing magic, it requires a great deal of skill, focus and determination. The mind must be free from whatever personal drama typically plagues it.

Scrying is like enhanced meditation. Instead of wandering through your own mind, a person must relax and allow the subconscious to take over. When our hidden thoughts surface to replace tedious conscious concerns, time drifts away allowing a peek into the future, the past and especially different areas of the future.

Past

Past life recalls, or scrying to remember forgotten events is like finding a key for an antique lock. The information is there. It's waiting. It just needs the right mechanism to present the answer.

I've found that when I stop trying to recall memories forgotten and focus on something simple, like watching wood burn, visions float before my eyes as if they lived there all along. The trick is to find focus in simplicity. This prepares the inner workings of one's depths to let answers fly.

Humans are complex creatures. We rely too much on the spoken word and thus fail to retain all the magnificent ideas that appear. Staring into flames, a mirror, smoke or crystal, links our immaterial thoughts to the physical world and gives them the weight they need to be purged from our subconscious.

Control is difficult. Scrying does not know time, so to look into the past, a person must have that purpose present in mind while also allowing themselves to give up full control over their thoughts.

Future

Looking ahead is similar to looking back, only chanting is highly encouraged. Because the future is not certain, it is more difficult to see. Everything that comes to someone while scrying is subject to change.

I glimpse the future in my dreams and when staring out of windows, so my preferred method of fire scrying is useless in this instance. When staring out into the world my eyes have a tendency to wander to my reflection. In that faint outline, I have spied things to come and things currently unfolding.

The first time it happened I was on the school bus coming home from school when I was maybe seven or eight years old. A horridly vivid scene of my father cheating on my mother played before my eyes. My young mind didn't know how to process it. I knew a little about reproduction and sex having been an avid reader of biology and nature books, but what my mind conjured disgusted me. It left me sick to my stomach for days.

Blinking through the glass, I smacked the surface and it disappeared. I never told my mother. I didn't have to. My father's indiscretions became known and were a constant blight on our family life for years until my parents divorced nearly ten years later.

Taking care to prepare for what might be revealed is pertinent. No matter how capable I am of handling bad news, there are some truths that take their toll. Be ready. That is the main lesson anyone who thinks they wish to scry should know.

Present

No matter how prepared I think I am, some visions are overwhelming. This is why the act of scrying is helpful. Instead of waking at random or being bombarded by images, scrying trains a person to repress those natural abilities until the time is right. It is ritualistic.

To sit and openly call upon visions is much more comfortable and affirming than to have them pop up like demented nightmares. But expectations must be realistic. It may sound silly to speak of science and realism in a book that discusses spirituality, but it is relevant.

At one time, curing a person with herbs was considered magic. Igniting gun powder was sorcery. I see no difference in exploring the undefined realms of our natural world and our connection to them. Scrying is not a science as defined by society right now, but it does have scientific elements. It takes hypothesis, experimentation and a mind strong enough to draw sensible conclusions.

Not every scrying experience will be a success, but it can lead to more tests. This approach keeps me from abusing my powers. Instead of looking to it as a magical aid for all things confusing, I practice this technique in moderation.

I have seen the past and the future, but most often I see what is currently happening away from me. When away from a loved one, or concerned for an ailing family member in the hospital, scrying draws forth images of their predicament at the time I'm seeking answers.

These images are real. They provide troubling and sometimes frustrating glimpses unseen. It makes me feel like a stalker or peeping Tom. There is little satisfaction unless connecting me to my husband or children.

The Act

There is not one way to look into the unseen. Scrying is just one method with many techniques. For anyone who wishes to have a manual laid out, I must regrettably apologize. All I can offer is a few steps based on my personal triumphs.

Step 1: Clear your space.
Whether outside by a fire or in a small room with just a mirror, it's important to be relaxed and feel secure, have time, etc.

Step 2: Clear your thoughts and focus on your object.
Fire, smoke, steam: whatever it is, let your conscious mind go numb. Then think of what you seek. Only that. Focus on staring into your crystal or watching the flames and let them dance with the idea of finding your past, looking into the future or seeing something hidden in the present.

Step 3: Don't force it.
Visions may come, or they may not. Sit and be patient. If enough time passes that the mind begins to wander, then finish and try at another time.

Step 4: Let what comes play out undaunted.

Try not to cry out or disturb the vision. That will end it. This is not always controllable as the body often enters a trance to allow the subconscious to take over but, if possible, avoid exclamations or outbursts.

I find silence to be the best aid, but chanting is okay. Light repetitive words are meditative. Also do not be afraid to move gently. I rock back and forth when a vision occurs. Sometimes I lean forward or slowly reach out.

It is an emotionally taxing experience, one that requires a person to relinquish control while still focusing. These ideas seem conflicting and that is why scrying is not easily performed.

Whatever the outcome, scrying holds power. It can aid guidance like the tarot or fool people into fearing the unknown. A balance must always be kept. Trusting one's self and the forces that created them helps keep a person safe while performing this task.

It is similar to spell-work in that regard. "Playing" with spells or scrying "for fun" can lead to misinterpretations or complications that have lasting effects. These methods are only solutions when all tangible options have been extinguished.

Spell-work

I don't take spells lightly. They can lose control, cause damage, or turn on their originator if not properly executed. When a person is spiritually balanced, they do not need to perform these rites often, I save them for when it really matters.

Like the Christians who tell children not to "waste their prayers" begging for gifts and material objects, I too see the merit in moderation. One who asks for less, receives more. There is only so much the universe can do for an individual after all.

But it is not all seriousness. Some spells are lighthearted. I've laughed through ritual and joked during certain spells. Remembering the purpose doesn't mean a person has to forget their sense of humor. It just means that people should be conscious of potential repercussions and selective of when they must expel their energies for a greater purpose.

Most of us believe in "the greater good." But what is "good" for some may not be considered so by another. This is why I so often speak of balance. Balanced spells will not shift tides or swing pendulums that should not be swung.

The question of free will comes to mind. In monotheism, followers are taught that humans were given free will. I agree that we are free to act as we choose to some degree but that the Gods, the universe, Mother Nature; everything that connects us, guides our hand no matter how hard we fight to disprove what cannot be seen.

To be wholly self-aware one must give in to the unknown. We must accept that, no matter how advanced society becomes, no matter how far we drive education and the quest for answers to life's questions, we will never know everything. We were not meant to know everything.

I once had a friend pose a question about defunding NASA. She joked about how people would change their tune when an asteroid hits the Earth. I jokingly retorted, "I don't know. Maybe the survival of other lives on other planets is contingent on the death of our planet and everything upon it."

I love life, I don't wish for anyone to mistake my meaning. I'm so desperately attached to this planet that I could never leave it even if that were possible. My husband often teases that he will pry me from the atmosphere if it were our only chance for survival. But when it comes to matters of "the greater good," I am not so presumptuous to believe that I or any other person in existence knows what is best for everyone. Death does not frighten me and neither does the unknown.

What frightens me is people who are so convinced they know everything; people who will argue one side of a point without even venturing to try and understand any opposition: people who divide, people who pick fights, people who dehumanize anyone unlike them.

Pagans and witches have suffered like any other people in history, but certain teachings have survived – the main one being, the ability to save one's self. That is what spell-work is made for. It is physical prayer. It has the power to shift things or aid a practitioner's mentality.

Like prayer, it is subjective.

Unlike monotheistic teachings, it gives people the power to look to themselves instead of begging the Gods for help. They have enough to tend to (in my experience).

So how do spells work?

How does one gain control over a spell?

It is important to master the Sabbats, full moon rituals and meditations before performing spells, so it is less out-of-the-ordinary. Spells are highly connected to all the rites. They begin and end much the same way. The details are somewhat different, but hold a similar sacredness.

Spell-work has three main aspects: building energy, the rite and grounding. It is best to start small and build up from there. These workings are not difficult to execute in theory, but they do change and sometimes drain the body and the mind.

Building Energies

To combat fatigue and cast a spell strong enough to work, preparation matters. Meditation and eating well should be standard, but the body needs some tending as well. Taking a bath cleanses the body to aid the soul. Utilizing the power of specific oils or bath salts can also get a person in the right mindset.

When done enjoying the power of water and stepping through the steam, clothing matters. I was raised to believe it shouldn't matter what a person wears, just as one should never be judged by their skin color or eye color, clothing seemed less important. I still hold to treating everyone with a friendly manner no matter what they wear, but clothing does set a tone.

There is a reason people wear costumes for stage plays or why ballerinas still wear tutus. What covers the body, what is present in a person's physical world, is a reflection of themselves. Being the silly butterfly that I am, I'm always clothed in bright colors. On rare occasions, I wear white or black but often with some eye-popping nail polish or a rainbow coat.

I do not subscribe to the self-righteous belief that everyone should dress like me or the naïve idea that income levels are not an issue. Having come from a life of poverty, I wish for more people to find the joy of thrift store shopping and second hand delights.

Some people choose to cast spells in the nude. I'm a lover of free skin. My feet hate shoes. Shoes are like prison cells for the feet. But they are helpful during winter, extreme heat and bee season (the only time I've ever been stung was when walking through a field and accidentally stepped on a bee hiding in a flower. I felt terrible for the poor thing and had to pluck it from my foot as it was still attached. No matter how lightly a person steps, they cannot avoid some tragedies).

I prefer floor length dresses. Organic cotton is the most comfortable, breathable fabric that dances with the wind. Men are encouraged to wear robes, kilts or whatever they wish, so long as it gives respect to the rite.

Rites

Every spell is different. Like people, they contain their own defining characteristics, but hold some similarities. No matter how many materials or thoughts a person wishes to convey in their spell, they need to know it inside and out. Research it. Feel it out. Trust all instincts.

If something doesn't feel right, it's not a good idea. A proper spell will call to the person meant to perform it. Once ready, banish all skepticism. Go into it with all the energy possible.

Follow every step strictly. This is not a time to test the rules. That will either prevent it from working or potentially misdirect the energies. Be sensitive to the nature of what's being done, but also relax and trust the subconscious. It may take over and guide any and all words spoken.

Have no fear. Trust in the rite. Then relax and cool off the energies with a simple grounding celebration.

Grounding

Grounding is how witches and Pagans keep themselves safe. Magic invites many unknown truths. It can empower, but if misplaced it can corrupt. Corruption creates imbalance and imbalances lead to harm.

To truly close a ceremony, even after finishing the work, grounding brings the spirit down form the natural high which spell-work brings. There are many ways to ground one's self but the main theme is reconnecting with the physical world with such practices as:

1. Laying on a bare floor and letting the powers drain back into the ground.

2. Pressing hands against a tree and looking up to the branches while the energies even out.

3. Sitting beside a trusted familiar and petting their fur, feathers or scales.

4. Writing about the experience of the spell.

5. Having sex with someone you care about (meaningless physical exertions often keep the ego inflated and don't allow a person to truly connect with their place in the world).

Practice

There is much to learn, and even more to ponder, but when put into play, spell-work is just another aspect of life. It is best to start with trusted sources. Scott Cunningham and Gerina Dunwich were my favorite early go-tos. From there, a world opened up and I now create my own spells based on my energies and my connection with nature and humanity.

"Practice" truly does "make perfect." Failure may occur, but that should never be a deterrent for a person who has their priorities in order. What everyone should know before they attempt spell-work is that they will need to bless a small basin of water, salt and cast a circle around their alter for protection.

I carve symbols into all my ritual candles. A picture of the Horned God for the Gods candle and the symbol of the Mother Goddess for the Goddesses candle. Then I picture that which pertains to what I am trying to effect on the purpose candle.

My Spells

Here are the successful spells I have created and found truth in (the spells of others come in handy when just beginning, or needing more sound assistance in your workings):

Water Blessing for Ritual

Fill a small bowl or container with water, place hands on the rim at opposite sides and dip fingers in. Focus energies on the great element of water and chant about its power and necessity.

Example:
> *Water powerful*
> *Water great*
> *Protect us on this sacred day*

Charging Salt for Ritual

Sprinkle an ample pile of salt on a small plate or in a container, place hands on either side and press fingertips atop. Focus energies on this earthy neutralizer, chant about its balance if needed, but closing your eyes and letting your energies flow is usually enough.

Chant to Help a Dying Soul Move On

Clear mind and focus energies. Feel them build with power, heat. Build until pressure is ready to burst then push out through a chant of letting the body rest and the soul move on.

Example:
> *Let his/her/its soul rest*
> *Let his/her/its body lie*
> *So that he/she/it can be ready*
> *For another existence in another time*

Repeat the chant over and over. Let the words build like a symphony and connect to the dying being. When energies are spent, allow silence to calm the air and take over, leading to the end.

Fall Sun Spell

In autumn, when wishing to feel the Sun's rays on a cloudy or rainy day, go outside and find a yellow or orange leaf (to represent the Sun). Hold it up to the sky, raising both arms and look to the clouds. Focus on separating their cover. Imagine the clouds move under the power while moving arms apart as if pushing them aside.

Say chant of bringing the Sun forth.

Example:
> *Clouds part right*
> *Now today*
> *Clouds part left*
> *Now today*
> *To open up to the power*
> *Of the Sun's rays*

This is a momentary spell that may not last long, depending on the energies. Not all clouds may part, but some should lighten to offer more beams through. (Always be careful when interfering with the nature of weather)

Pendant Protection Spell

Set the altar facing north. Place the Gods and Goddesses candles next to each other at the head. Set the purpose candle (colored to the need, or white for all-purpose) in between but further down – like the point of a triangle.

Place the pendant on the altar before the purpose candle. Light the Gods candle and welcome the male aspects of being. Light the Goddesses candle and welcome the female attributes. Then light the purpose candle and create a chant of protection.

Something from the heart.

Personal if for self or about the intended if for someone else.

Example:

>*Connect our energies*
>*So that (I/person intended)*
>*Can draw strength*
>*And be protected*

Dangle the pendant on its chain or cord over the purpose candle and let it sway in the flame. Continue chanting until you cannot anymore.

Place the pendant before the candles once more and bow to it. Leave the candles to burn out. Then wear it. The chain or cord will break or fall off when the spell relinquishes its hold.

Curse Breaking Crochet

Crochet a clothing item such as a hat, gloves or socks, for the person under the power of a curse. Chant something specific to end that situation and repeat it while looping each stitch. When finished, hug the garment and then gift it to the person under the curse.

Example:

>*By the power of three*
>*Let the curse break free*
>*Let it die down*
>*And let love bloom in this weave*

Leaf Protection Spell *(To Guide a Changing Friendship)*

Find three leaves and gather with a basin of blessed water. Place on the altar before the north-facing Gods and Goddesses candles. Set the purpose candle before the basin to form the point of a triangle with the candles and the basin in the center.

Take the first leaf and place it in the water while chanting about the situation.

Example:

> *Protect our friendship*
> *Let it float always*
> *Like a light leaf*
> *Like a boat on the tide*

While chanting, drip the purpose candle over the leaf. Repeat this with the other two leaves. When all three are covered, chant and drip wax between to connect them as they dry.

> *Bow forehead to basin and dip fingers in the water, still chanting.*
> *Brush fingertips over the wax to seal the spell and end the chant.*

Candle Talents Spell *(to Aid Creativity)*

Set altar facing north with one candle to represent the Gods and one to represent the Goddesses at the head. Place the candle of your purpose in the middle of the altar. Then set a necklace around the purpose candle to connect them.

Cast a circle by walking clockwise and sprinkling salt with each step, using your right hand. Do this three times around while asking the Gods to be present and bless the rite.

Then pick up the water container and sprinkle some drops around the circle, going counter-clockwise while flinging drops with your left hand. Do this three times around.

Light the Gods and Goddesses candles and thank them for your talents. Then light the purpose candle and chant about drawing strength from within to continue learning and improving in your special talent.

Example:

> *Writing is my strength*
> *It keeps me healthy*
> *Keeps me sane*
> *Writing is my strength*
> *Protect my writing*
> *And all its practices*

Then pick up the necklace and dangle it over the purpose candle three times clockwise right-handed, and three times counter-clockwise left handed. Focus your energies into the necklace, then place it around your neck, hold, or give it to the person you are performing the spell for. Meditate and visualize moving forward with said talent.

Protection from Harassment

Place the altar facing north with one Gods candle and one Goddesses candle at the head and a chalice of wine in between. Set a purpose candle in the center with salt and water beside it. Place a piece of paper before it. Place a dagger to the left of it and a pen to the right.

Cast a circle with the salt and water, walking and chanting to welcome the Gods.

Light the Gods candles and chant for their aid. State the issue and light the purpose candle. Then chant for the person in need of protection.

Example:

> *Get (name) through the dark days*
> *Get (name) through the misty haze*
> *Get (name) to their next phase*
> *Get (name) through this waning phrase*
> *Let (name) be free from their pain*
> *Let (name) be free from this harassment*

*Write the name of the person being harassed next to the name of the person harassing them. Circle the names **individually**. Fold the paper in half and chant to protect the person from the harasser.*

Example:

> *Protect (name) though this moon's phase*
> *So (name) will be free*
> *And give (name's) antagonist*
> *Clarity and peace*
> *So they will leave (name) be*

Fold the paper in half again (so quartered) and chant for the harasser

Example:
>   *Give him/her clarity and peace*
>   *So he/she will leave (name) be*

Now take up the paper. Open it and rip between the circled names to symbolize the distancing of the two people. Burn each piece individually, the harassed's using the appropriate Gods or Goddess candle and the harasser using the purpose candle. Chant a binding to seal the spell.

Example:
>   *Protect (name)*
>   *Give (harasser) a new direction*
>   *Give (name) their freedom*
>   *And offer (harasser) peace*

Make sure all of each name burns.

Once charred, close by thanking the Gods/powers that be. Dip fingers (one per candle) in God or Goddess candle and smear on cheeks. Open the circle.

Note: name may take a while to burn, especially if both parties are struggling to let go of their frustration. May need to reignite paper and/or chant of letting go as well).

Full Moon Increase Confidence

Perform on the morning of the full moon. Go outside at dawn while the birds are singing their best. Meditate.

Clear the mind and focus on the birdsong. Feel the energies connect between self and nature. Hum with the tune to better relax.

Then lift up your voice and sing or chant about your own role in the universe.

Example:
>*I am not a name*
>*I am my spirit*
>*I am not a name*
>*I am my energies*
>*But through my name*
>*People feel me*
>*My spirit*
>*And my energies*

Rite to Save a Child

Set the altar facing north. Place the Gods and Goddess candles at the head. Place a candle representing the child at the bottom of the altar, making it the point of a large triangle. Inside of the space between candles, fill the altar with emotionally charged items – as many as possible: the child's toys, clothing, books, pictures of the kid, a piece of paper with their name, birth date and best qualities written on it.

Open with a blessing on the life that hangs in the balance and light the candles. Envision and focus energies on helping that child to pull through (this is a transference, the image of an elderly loved one or family member will be brought forth, this is the person who will sacrifice their life for the child).

Let the spell guide a chant to connect the elderly's sacrifice to the child so the energies are properly transferred. This is a very draining spell. **It can only save a person at the loss of another within a certain time frame.**

Example: If the child is said to have six months to live, the spell will exchange deaths to the elderly person linked to the spell through the chant at the time the child would have died. The balance must be kept. This spell cannot be twisted. Death is impossible to avoid. **Do NOT perform unless absolutely necessary.**

Chant until unable to. Then bow to the Gods, thank nature for her aid and let the candles burn out.

Spiritual Journey

Life's journeys never end. Even the least flawed human is imperfect. We are meant to continue growing and changing no matter how far we get.

Living a spiritually connected life means feeling more, experiencing everything to the depths of one's being. It is more painful at times but also much more joyous, and never boring. It also means valuing questions, opposing viewpoints, and intelligent discourse.

Anyone who wishes to silence those who express differing beliefs is stagnant. They cannot flourish beyond their preconceived notions. This does not mean they should be vilified or shamed. How we find our way is based on who we are, where we come from and what we perceive. The best way to combat ignorance is by walking away from those who refuse to see light and promoting better behaviors.

But one cannot always avoid certain blockers. Society puts rules and laws in place for "the greater good," that sometimes harm our collective growth. I believe in truth, honesty and justice. Those are the foundations I built my life upon, but sometimes I find contradictions within our system; mainly in legislation against natural substances that enhance the spirit and connect people through our shared powers.

To be clear, I do not condone breaking the law. It is never a good idea to tempt fate. Respect is a two-way street that one must always extend first. I've walked some of the roughest neighborhoods at night without incident because of the respect I gave to those who are often looked down upon.

I am an individualist at heart and treat others as such. But there is plenty of evidence that certain natural aids enhance our minds and spirits. Marijuana and psychedelics in mushroom form have been subject to much propaganda. From when the paper mill moguls wished to destroy the hemp industry to retain their profits, to fearful governments that banned all psychedelics when the LSD epidemic of the late sixties exploded, not all illegal substances deserve their bans.

Prohibition proved to be a failure and as many U.S. states remove their penalties for marijuana use, one can only hope that natural psychedelics will get a second chance to aid humanity in our evolution.

Our knowledge of the medicinal benefits of consuming marijuana continues to expand. The list of health problems this single plant protects people from continues to grow. It is less addictive than most prescribed options with little to no side-effects.

To-date marijuana is known to combat:

Agitation of Alzheimer's
Anxiety
Arthritis
Autism
Bipolar Disorder
Cachexia
Cancer
Cerebral Palsy
Crohn's Disease
Chronic Pain
Cystic Fibrosis
Diabetes
Ehler's Danlos Syndrome
Epidermolysis Bullosa
Epilepsy
Fibromyalgia
Glaucoma
Hepatitis C
HIV/AIDS

Huntington's Disease
Inflammatory Bowel Disease (IBD)
Lou Gehrig's Disease
Lupus
Migraines
Mitochondrial Disease
Multiple Sclerosis
Muscle Spasms
Muscular Dystrophy
Nausea
Obstructive Sleep Apnea
Parkinson's Disease
PTSD
Sickle Cell Disease
Spasticity
Traumatic Brain Injury (TBI)
Tourette's Syndrome
Ulcerative Colitis

This is the short list. It grows as more research is done. There is a reason people consider marijuana a miracle plant.

When the body is healthy, the spirit shines. Utilizing this aid can gift Pagans and witches with serenity. It can clear the mind and allow singular focus to prepare for ritual, guided meditation or spell-work. It can open the third eye and allow for more successful scrying.

Magical mushrooms and cactus juice go further. Instead of relaxing the mind, they utilize areas of the brain that are thought to be more dormant. This opens new ideas, revelations; a gateway to a more connected self who sees the direct links to their role in the world.

Wine is my natural antidepressant. When I need help controlling the darker side of my bipolar, a glass of wine softens the edges and reminds me of the romance in existence. It eases my brain and soothes my nerves.

When used in moderation, these natural elements provide balanced insights. They gift the soul with doorways to other realms of thought. They can help seekers find solutions from within.

Unfortunately, like all nutrients when abused, the body rebels. One must be able to take days, weeks and months off in order to find that balance. Enhancers are not a whole life, they should never become routine. It sullies the experience and dampens the brain to the freedom.

Alcoholism runs in my family. I know it lives in me. I could easily drink wine all day every day. I know this and I keep strict watch over my actions because I have no interest in destroying my liver. When I start to crave wine for my breakfast, I know I've been having it too often and enforce a sober month. A full month of sobriety reminds me to appreciate myself and the world around me without padding.

It is not easy. It hurts sometimes. But the necessity is stronger than ever.

Cactus juice and magical mushrooms give people their visions and help them "trip" due to toxins. This means users are giving themselves small amounts of poison to free the mind. That's quite a quest for knowledge.

The long-term effects of over use of these substances are:

High blood pressure
Constant twitching or shaking
Loss of muscle control
Poor coordination.

Basically, all the things correlate to burnouts. The philosophy of "take only what you need," stands true here. No matter how spiritual a person becomes, they still need to be present in the physical world. Overuse of psychedelics is not soulful, it is escapism.

People often sell escapism as a lifestyle because they cannot cope with the world as it is. That leads to destructive behavior for themselves or others. When one cannot differentiate between reality and fantasy, then they create chaos and suffering. That is the opposite of what I am detailing.

Abuse is partly where my pharmacaphobia originated. I was never a druggie, but I did drink a bit in my teens. At sixteen I thought I could safely get drunk. A group of friends and I hung out at one friend's house and his parents supervised us during our immature binges.

But no matter how much the booze made me forget about my unstable home life or my uncertain future, it always wore off. When the peak is over, the fall hits hard (at least with bi-polars like me). I found myself over analyzing everything. There was no support, not love, no warmth. My friends didn't take me seriously and often underestimated my intelligence because of my silly nature.

I would always rather laugh than cry, but the tears build up. Sometimes they turn into monsters. They haunt anyone who keeps them inside. I found myself alone in the bathroom with a full medicine cabinet, glaring at myself in the mirror.

It seemed as if I was everyone's problem. I honestly felt that the world would be a better place without me. My mind was unhinged. The drinking didn't do it; it was coming off of the drinking that unleashed everything.

That's the problem with addictive substances, they make you feel good for a while but they wear off and it takes more and more to get back to that euphoria every time. They destroy people from the inside out, figuratively and literally.

I swallowed a bottle of pills ready to kiss myself goodbye.

After the drama of being found out, having my mom dragged out, going in and out of consciousness in the back of a speeding car, the hospital induced a lot of vomiting and I spent a week institutionalized with stomach pains, therapy and some factorized doctor trying to "cure" me with addictive meds.

That was the last thing I could face. I'm a fast learner. I knew I had made a mistake by the morning after I tried to kill myself. Convincing the doctors was an uphill battle, but a week later I was released.

I ran to the first patch of grass I saw and kissed it. I hugged my mom and her car. I vowed never to go back and so I have been strict about knowing my limits.

When used every once in a while, and legally (travel helps), natural aids and spiritual enhancing methods reveal hidden secrets that exist in nature. Self-awareness, health and balance make for a stronger life structure that give those who wish to expand their mind through natural enhancers the control they require to maintain balance, even when relinquishing power over their consciousness.

Thank You (Conclusion)

If you've read as far as this, you're almost finished. I want to say thank you for taking the time to listen to my insights. I hope that I have given enough information for a start.

Please meditate. Get in touch with nature. Life is always living.

Celebrate. Learn and grow without fear of failure. Acceptance from others comes from self-awareness and the connections we bridge.

Fate is waiting. She can heal. She is unpredictable, but not unkind. There are futures to be met, spells to empower and enhancers to witness. Whatever you gather from this book and carry with you in your heart, remember that your path is your own.

Your instincts are waiting. Buried inside, they are crying to be heard. Listening, absorbing their wisdom is an art. Embrace this gift and let it lift up your smile.

Helpful resources

The Witches' Voice: http://www.witchvox.com/

The St. Louis Pagan Picnic: http://www.paganpicnic.org/

Circle Sanctuary: https://www.circlesanctuary.org/

Chicago Pagan Pride: http://www.chicagopaganpride.org/

The Seattle Metaphysical Library: http://www.seattlemetaphysicallibrary.org/

Witches and Pagans Magazine: www.witchesandpagans.com

Works Cited

Cloud, Cam. "The Little Book of Acid." Ronin Publishing. 20 Jan, 1999. Print.

Crowley, Aleister. "The Book of the Law." Weiser Books. 1909. Print.

Cunningham, Scott. "The Complete Book of Incense, Oils and Brews." Llewellyn's Practical Magic. 2 Sept, 2002. Print.

Cunningham, Scott. "Earth, Air, Fire, & Water: More Techniques of Natural Magic." Llewellyn's Practical Magic. 8 Sept, 2002. Print.

Cunningham, Scott. "Living Wicca: A Further Guide for the Solitary Practitioner." Llewellyn's Practical Magic. 8 Sept, 2002. Print.

Cunningham, Scott. "Wicca: A Guide for the Solitary Practitioner." Llewellyn Publications. 1989. Print.

Desert Hope Treatment Staff. "What Are the Long-Term Effects of Using Psychedelic Mushrooms?" Desert Hope. 3 May, 2018. Web. https://deserthopetreatment.com/psychedelic-mushrooms/long-term-effects/

Dunwich, Gerina. "Exploring Spellcraft: How to Create and Cast Effective Spells." New Page Books. 1 Nov, 2001. Print.

Dunwich, Gerina. "Wicca Craft: The Modern Witches Book of Herbs, Magic and Dreams." Library of the Mystic Arts. 1 Jun, 2000. Print.

Eagleman, David. "Incognito: The Secret Lives of the Brain." Pantheon Books. 31 May, 2011. Print.

Kaldera, Raven & Schwartzstein, Tannin. "Handfastings and Wedding Rituals: Welcoming Hera's Blessing." Llewellyn Publications. 8 Dec, 2003. Print.

Leek, Sybil. "Diary of a Witch." Signet Publishing. 1 Jul, 1969. Print.

Dr. Rosado, Joseph. "Medical Conditions Treatable with Marijuana." Marijuana Doctors. 30 Jan, 2019. Web. https://www.marijuanadoctors. com/conditions/

Smith, Lori. "10 Most Common Birth Control Pill Side Effects." Medical News Today. 29, Jan 2018. Web. https://www.medicalnewstoday.com/ articles/290196.php

Wenner, Melinda. "Birth Control Pills Affect Women's Taste in Men." Scientific American. 1 Dec, 2008. Web. https://www.scientificamerican. com/article/birth-control-pills-affect-womens-taste/